HEAT UP YOUR HOT SCENES

L.A. WITT

CONTENTS

Copyright Information

This is a work of fiction. Names, characters, places, and incidents are either the product of the author's imagination or are used fictitiously. Any resemblance to actual persons living or dead, business establishments, events, or locales is entirely coincidental.

Heat Up Your Hot Scenes

First edition

Copyright © 2023 L.A. Witt

Cover Art by Lori Witt

Books quoted within the text are used with authors' permission. All rights retained by the authors.

All rights reserved. No part of this book may be reproduced or transmitted in any form or by any means, electronic or mechanical, including photocopying, record ing, or by any information storage and retrieval system without the written permission of the publisher, and where permitted by law. Reviewers may quote brief passages in a review. To request permission and all other inquiries, contact L.A. Witt at gallagherwitt@gmail.com

Ebook ISBN: 978-1-64230-158-8

Paperback ISBN: 979-8-39983-546-4

Hardcover ISBN: 979-8-85891-550-8

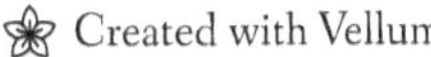 Created with Vellum

ARTIFICIAL INTELLIGENCE

No artificial intelligence was used in the making of this book or any of my books. This includes writing, co-writing, cover artwork, translation, and audiobook narration.

I do not consent to any Artificial Intelligence (AI), generative AI, large language model, machine learning, chatbot, or other automated analysis, generative process, or replication program to reproduce, mimic, remix, summarize, train from, or otherwise replicate any part of this creative work, via any means: print, graphic, sculpture, multimedia, audio, or other medium. This applies to all existing AI technology and any that comes into existence in the future.

I support the right of humans to control their artistic works.

HEAT UP YOUR HOT SCENES

Love scenes are arguably some of the most difficult scenes to write. How do you keep each scene from sounding the same? Where is the line between too real and too far into fantasy? Which words and euphemisms will work with your tone, and which will kill the mood? When should you show every camera angle? When should you fade to black?

There's a lot to it, and a well-written love scene can make or break a story. No pressure, right?

Award-winning romance author L.A. Witt is here to help! After 15 years, almost 200 titles, and at least 1,000 sex scenes, she's run into every pitfall and brick wall imaginable… and she's found solutions to most of them!

With focus on technique—both yours *and* your characters'—*Heat Up Your Hot Scenes* covers all the bases from choosing the right word to dialing up the emotional intensity to things that might inadvertently make your readers wince.

Heat Up Your Hot Scenes is an inclusive, LGBTQ+ friendly guide to writing hot, emotional, humorous, and even suspenseful love scenes to keep your readers turning pages and coming back for more.

INTRODUCTION

Just who do I think I am?

If you're reading this book, I'm going to make an assumption about you. Specifically, that you're writing erotic and/or romantic fiction and would like to either learn how to write sex scenes or improve the sex scenes you're currently writing (read: make them sexier, hotter, more erotic, etc.).

That, or you're one of my friends or family members who's curious about what I write and wants to know how this whole thing works, but who doesn't want to actually pick up one of my novels, and you are hoping I don't use any personal anecdotes in this book.

I'm also going to assume that you have a certain expectation about me. Namely, that I know what the heck I'm talking about. So, this is the part where I get into who I am and why on earth I think I have any authority or expertise on this subject. If you're familiar with me and my work, it won't hurt my feelings if you skip this section, though you might want to stick around in case I throw out some one-liner to make you choke on your coffee. I'm in this to educate and entertain, y'all.

All of which is a long-winded way of landing here: I'm L.A. Witt. I'm also Lauren Gallagher, Ann Gallagher, and Lori A. Witt. Ann and Lori don't write much smut, but L.A. and Lauren do, and have since 2008.

As the combined quad, I am a recipient of the Romance Writers of America Centennial Award for 100 Published Novels. I'm the author or co-author of around 200 novels and novellas, plus a handful of short stories. Most of them are on the erotic end of the spectrum, though I've also written sweet and even inspirational romances. Many of my titles are award winners, including winning the EPIC Award for Erotica two years in a row (2016 & 2017), the Passionate Plume Award's Contemporary Erotic Romance category three years in a row (2014, 2015, & 2016), and finaling in the Lambda Literary Awards six times. I've also won the National Leather Association's Pauline Reage Novel Award, and have medaled four times in the Independent Publisher Book Awards Erotica category—two silvers and a bronze on my own, and a gold with Anna Zabo.

With that many books under my belt (erm, so to speak), my *conservative* estimate is that I've written over 1,000 sex scenes in the last 15 years. They run the gamut when it comes to sexuality—I have written gay, bisexual, heterosexual, and lesbian sex scenes, ranging from vanilla to kinky. I've written everything from solo masturbation scenes to group sex involving half a dozen participants, and my characters have played with floggers, handcuffs, strap-ons, sex machines, and dildos. They've fooled around in cars, boats, strip clubs (including lapdances!), alleys, offices, kitchens, and even the locker room of a fencing club. So... you could say I've got some experience!

And the thing is, even now I find sex scenes very challenging to write. If you think they're tough, you're not alone —it isn't easy to keep them hot, fresh, and interesting from one to the next.

But it can be done, and that's why I've written this book.

What are you going to learn from this book?

The short answer is... how I keep my erotic scenes hot, sexy, and believable.

Wait, why would you want your sex scenes to be believable? It's fiction!

Of course it is. And there's an element of fantasy, of course. As both a reader and a writer, though, I find that a degree of realism makes the story more, well, real. The scene will be more vivid and intense, and it'll engage the reader more, just like giving a character flaws makes them more real. Even if there's vampires involved, or they're getting it on in the back of a spaceship on the way to another galaxy, the sex—and the emotions, the sensations, the connection between the characters—will be real. It'll pull the reader in closer, and the scene will stay with them long after the sheets have cooled.

I'm going to cover a lot of ground in this book. I'll get into everything from whether your characters need to use condoms, how different word choices can affect the entire tone of the scene, how much realism is *too* much realism, and how to write things that squick *you* out without squicking out your reader (it can be done, I promise!).

As I mentioned above, most of what you learn in this

book will be based on how I approach sex scenes. That generally comes from trial and error, things I've liked and disliked when reading erotica, and feedback from readers, reviewers, and editors. I am not an infallible expert, and you may not find all of my advice useful. It's just that—advice. Take what works and ignore the rest.

Throughout, you will find many examples of my advice in action since that's the best way to show what I'm talking about. The majority of the examples I use are from my own work simply because they're accessible to me. It's certainly not "my sex scenes are the greatest ever," but rather "here's an example to illustrate the point I'm making." Passages from other authors' work are used with permission; at the end of the book, you'll find a list of those books and links to the authors' websites.

It goes without saying that these excerpts are often explicitly sexual.

And some disclaimers...

1. Nearly every example or piece of advice in this book can be challenged with "but sometimes in real life..." or "but what if my story..." And that's okay. I'm speaking in pretty general terms because if I discuss every exception and variation, this book will be 7,000 pages long. For example, there are people who dislike giving or receiving oral sex. I don't mention them in the areas where I discuss oral because it's assumed and implied that we're talking about characters who *are* into it.
2. Similarly, every piece of advice includes the caveat "...unless you're going for something else, in which case, this doesn't apply." If I say "You

don't want your reader to be crossing their legs and cringing," but that's exactly what you're going for, then that piece of advice doesn't apply. Assume at every turn that I'm speaking in general terms with the full awareness that every sex scene, character, writer, and book is different.

3. This is also why I have not included exceptions or sidebars for paranormal, science fiction, or other-than-contemporary-Earth situations because… well, there are simply way too many variables, and there's no way I could contain all possibilities within the scope of this book. Suffice it to say, some things I say in this book can be countered with "but in my universe…". That's okay.

4. In a number of places, I'll get into significant detail about things that you may decide are not an issue. There's a chapter that gets into the logistics of sex on the beach. You may very well come to the conclusion that I'm overthinking things, and reject my advice. Or you may have zero desire whatsoever to write sex on the beach, in which case you're welcome to skip the chapter (or read it and see if anything is useful in other areas). There is no final exam and no one watching over your shoulder to make sure you read every word. Promise.

5. I'm going to talk a lot about planning. This can be interpreted however you wish, from just giving a scene some forethought to creating a detailed outline. If you're a true pantser who doesn't plan ahead, then "planning" in this book

can be interpreted as simply as just thinking about your story or what you have in mind while you're writing an otherwise unplanned scene. Most of what I suggest can be adapted to any writing process, but as always, take what works and ignore the rest.

So, basically I'm going to explain how I approach sex scenes, and offer advice for you to do the same. Some of it may be useful to you, some of it may not, and some of it may work after you've adapted it to fit your own process and writing. Whatever the case, hopefully you'll find a few things in here that'll help heat up your own erotic fiction!

How this book is organized

The book is divided into two parts, and yes, I'm inordinately proud of this ridiculous alliteration:

1. Pacing, Porn, & Publishing: Your technique
2. Positions, Practices, & Prophylactics: Your characters' technique

Which is a very simple way of saying that the first half will focus on things like word choice, pacing, tone, and research, while the second half will get into the specifics of what your characters are doing on the page.

The chapters don't need to be read in order, so feel free to move around or skip chapters altogether if they're not useful to you.

A word about gender & sexual identity

I'm going to keep it light throughout most of this book, because... insert joke here about how nothing should be dry in a book about sex scenes.

But... I want to be serious for just a minute.

I have tried to be as inclusive as possible throughout the book, with examples taken from hetero, bi, lesbian, and gay scenes, and discussing sex in a variety of combinations. I have also done my best to take into consideration that sex (and sexy scenes) absolutely includes people who don't identify as cisgender male or female. Not everyone with a penis is a man and not everyone with a vagina is a woman, and it is not my intention to exclude any identity, so for the vast majority of the book, I use gender neutral pronouns (they/them).

Many of my examples will come from LGBTQ+ books, particularly M/M, because that's what I read and write, so I'm more likely to recall a scene from such a book when I need to make a point. By and large, the principles apply across genders and orientations.

One final thought before we get started.

There's one piece of writing advice that I've never liked: *if writing your sex scenes don't turn you on, they won't turn the reader on.*

I disagree with this for two reasons. First, because you might not share your characters' kinks or turn-ons. That doesn't mean you can't write a perfectly sexy and hot scene. I've written scenes with my characters doing things I would never in a million years do, but I'm not writing them from my point-of-view. I'm writing from my *characters'* point-of-view, and the characters would be turned on by it.

Second, you're not necessarily going to be turned on *while* you're writing. Writing is not easy, and writing sex—I mean, there's a reason you're reading this book, right? It's because writing sex scenes is a lot of work! If you're writing a scene with characters doing something that you find unbearably hot, but the process doesn't feel sexy and doesn't turn you on—that doesn't mean you're failing. It just means you're *writing*. When you read it afterward, you'll probably feel differently. (And if you don't, that's okay too—some people aren't turned on by their own work. Have a beta reader give it a read!)

It's a little like glamour photography, honestly. Ask any model or photographer, and they'll tell you the actual shoot is anything but sexy. Poses that look sexy in a photo don't feel sexy in the moment. Lights get hot. Photographers have to contort into a million positions to get just the right angle. Makeup smears. And that's to say nothing about all the editing and corrective work afterward—nothing sexier than staring at a computer screen and turning a bunch of pixels into something sexy, am I right?

The point is, the *result* needs to be sexy. The process does not.

So, with all of that in mind, let's proceed into the realms of writing hot, memorable sex scenes!

PART 1

PACING, PORN, & PUBLISHING: YOUR TECHNIQUE

CHAPTER 1

WHAT SHOULD A SEX SCENE ACCOMPLISH?

Off the cuff, the answer to that question seems pretty obvious.

In reality, though, it's not so simple. Not even close.

While sex scenes are often brushed off as gratuitous and serving no purpose beyond titillation, that couldn't be further from the truth. They certainly *can* be gratuitous, and they certainly *can* be without purpose, but that's not a result of being sex scene—that's a result of being, well, gratuitous and serving no purpose. Fight scenes and car chase scenes can be the same way.

So how does a writer avoid purposeless sex scenes? Quite frankly, by giving a sex scene a purpose. By making it something a reader can't skim without missing part of the story.

Okay, but *how?*

One of the most effective approaches is to give a sex scene an emotional component. If you're writing romance, you're going to want to have that component more often than not. It doesn't have to be something earth-shattering, either—just giving the characters some intimacy and bonding time to strengthen their relationship and push them toward their happy ending, for example, or giving them—and the reader—a break before the tension/action escalate.

Make your sex scene *mean* something. Maybe your characters have one last night (or less!) before parting ways. Maybe they need to say something to each other but can't find the words. Maybe the sex will be lackluster and without completion, revealing negative emotions one partner has been trying to keep from the other (What? You didn't think all the sex had to be explosive and perfect, did you? More on that later.).

Sex scenes can serve any number of purposes; the sky really is the limit.

I want to pause here and say that there is absolutely nothing wrong with writing sex scenes that exist solely for titillating the reader. This is where the line gets fuzzy between erotica and porn, though. There's nothing wrong with landing on either side of that line so long as you, the writer, are aware of and in control of where you land.

Are you writing a purely physical one-handed read to make your reader sweat? Awesome.

Do you want the reader to be turned on and out of breath but also emotionally invested? Great.

Just know what you want the scene to do to your reader before you go into it.

If you're setting out to write one-handed reads, you can probably skip the rest of this chapter.

If you're aiming for sex scenes that tap into readers' emotions, read on.

The simplest and most obvious way a sex scene can

have an emotional impact is by using it to further the relationship. The characters can be a little unsure and nervous in earlier scenes, then increasingly more comfortable with each other as time goes on. They can show their deepening trust by trying new things, or simply by being more confident and relaxed with each other. Or they can have an easy dynamic in the bedroom early on, but as the black moment looms, that dynamic falters, and the sex scene signals that there is trouble ahead.

And don't stop at bringing the characters closer or deepening their intimacy. Sex scenes are so spectacularly versatile. For example, as I touched on in the previous paragraph, a sex scene can foreshadow trouble between the characters. In real life, it's not unusual for a marriage counselor to ask a struggling couple about their sex life early on. How often are they having sex? How satisfied are they? This isn't because the solution to their problems is going to be "have more sex" or because a relationship with little to no sex is doomed—it's because sex is one of the places where a relationship's cracks begin to show. Resentment, guilt, lack of connection, tension—all of that is hard to hide, but it's even harder to hide in the bedroom.

So, in fiction, sex is a fantastic place to show that your characters are headed for troubled waters. Are they drifting apart? Show them going through the motions without much enthusiasm. Is one character worried the other is slipping away? Show them being unusually earnest in bed. Have them surprise the other by wearing something sexy or proposing a new bedroom activity. Is there something bothering a character so badly they can't focus? Are they conspicuously trying extra hard in bed, inadvertently revealing exactly what they're trying to hide (i.e., that they're scared, distracted, depressed, etc.)? Show them unable to perform, and show how that affects their partner —suspicion? Worry that *they're* the problem? The possibilities are endless, and those are just a few of the myriad ways a sex scene can show relationship problems.

In this example from my book *Kneel, Mr. President*, James and Carlene are desperately trying to hold on to their marriage. James knows something is wrong, but he can't get Carlene to tell him, so he tries another way to reconnect with her. And, well...

"I don't want to talk anymore," he whispered between kisses.

"Neither do I."

So they didn't talk. They climbed into bed, and her jersey, his boxers and her panties all eventually made their way onto the floor. James held her close, the warmth of her body turning him on and reassuring him that, yes, she really had come home, though every movement was slow and subdued, almost lethargic. Even as he moved inside her, it was like there was a layer of something between them. Like back in the days when they'd used condoms, only...more. Separating every place they tried to touch with something just thick enough to dull the senses and temper all the feverish heat.

He tried moving faster, thrusting harder, kissing her more passionately, but...nothing. He was turned on enough to stay hard, but at this rate, even that wasn't going to last much longer.

What the hell?

Beneath him, Carlene relaxed a little. Her arms loosened around him.

He slowed down. There had to be something he could do. Some way to turn her—

"I'm exhausted." She caressed his face. "It's been a long day. Maybe…"

Message received.

"Yeah." He fought to keep the resignation out of his voice, and he withdrew slowly. "Same here."

"Tomorrow night?"

"Definitely." He kissed her once more, then eased himself down beside her.

Neither of them spoke—what could they really say right then? James lay on his back. She lay on hers. His heart pounded in his ears. The city made all its nighttime noise in the distance. Between the two of them, though… Nothing.

- Kneel Mr. President

Similarly, sex can *help* with problems. That's not to say your characters will fix all their issues by rumpling the bedsheets together, but sometimes the body can find the words the brain can't. Whether it's getting someone's mind off something…

I didn't need to think about anything but the blowjob. The sweet, sweet blowjob. Jacob's rhythm picked up, and he started kneading my bare ass cheek with his free hand, the one that wasn't steadily jacking me toward my peak, just the right speed, not too fast, not too slow, just right, and his mouth was just right too, so wet, so good, and pretty soon I'd be spiraling toward that...

A car engine revved outside. Headlights shone through a gap in the mail slot. I caught my breath, loud. Jacob stilled and listened. Across the street, a storm door slammed.

False alarm. Just a neighbor. Unfortunately, the moment of panic had pushed me most of the way back to the starting gate. Jacob stood, still jacking my spit-wet dick. He ran his hand down my upper arm where it was still parked behind my head, petting me from protruding elbow to shoulder. With a smoldering look, he purred, "I *will* make you forget about whatever's bothering you."

"It's just..."

He fit his mouth to my ear and said, "A good, hard fuck is what you need."

- Spook Squad
From the PsyCop series
by Jordan Castillo Price

Or breaking some seemingly unbreakable tension...

Daniel clenched his jaw and pushed his shoulders back. "I still love you. Even now. Knowing what you are and why you're here. Happy?" He held his hands out to the sides. "So if you're still going to kill me," he said, his voice wavering, "would you just get it over with?"

I stared at him. I couldn't move. Speak. Breathe. The shine in his eyes, it . . . it was . . . Daniel *never* fucking cried.

"I . . ." Can't? Won't?

"I never set out to hurt you in any way," Daniel said, his voice cracking. "I hope you of all people know that. You can't ever have thought that I did what I did because I *wanted* you to suffer. I just couldn't sit back and watch you turn into a goddamned cyborg."

Anger surged to the surface, masking the ache that tried to rise in my throat. "And isn't it poetic that you fucking drove me to getting more mods than I ever wanted?"

"I drove you to that?" he snapped. He reached up and swiped at his eyes. "Bullshit. You were hooked just like any other mod junkie. You're half machine. You're a murderer. Vampire or not, are you even *remotely* human anymore?"

"You tell me."

I forced him up against the thick glass wall, and kissed him.

- *A Chip In His Shoulder*

In what I quoted above from *Spook Squad*, there's a lot of depth to what's going on in that scene. Vic (the POV character) is worried and distracted, and his partner is both worried about him and determined to help in one of the only ways he knows how. The whole scene is smoking hot, but make no mistake—there's much more to it than just a blowjob. There are *chapters* of tension leading up to it, and the sex is cathartic for the reader as well as the characters, not to mention building on the already strong relationship between Jacob and Vic.

Unlike Jacob and Vic, the boys in *A Chip in His Shoulder* are definitely not on any kind of stable ground. They're a couple of violently estranged exes, and one is a hitman who's literally been sent to kill the other. The sudden shift from fighting to kissing is both a tension breaker (the standoff is over) and a tension escalator (how is Daniel going to respond?). Strictly speaking, it's not a sex scene, but you get the idea—don't underestimate what a sexually charged moment can do for your characters and the tension between them.

This is in large part because sex makes people incredibly vulnerable. The sudden kiss above makes both men even more physically and emotionally vulnerable than they already were. Escalating to a full-on sex scene just amps that up. That's why it's so intimate, and sometimes it can be scary. Humans tend to fear the unknown, and when you combine that fear of the unknown with the vulnerability of sex, there will definitely be some emotions involved. Maybe your character is having sex for the first time ever. Or they've recently discovered they're bisexual and this is their first time with a man. Or maybe this is the first time since a bad experience with a previous partner, or the first time since an injury.

Maybe they're just afraid they won't be good at it.

Because our society puts such emphasis on a person's sexual prowess—and puts down people who aren't great in bed—there's tremendous pressure to perform. This can manifest in performance anxiety, of course, and because biology is a cruel thing, that performance anxiety can result in exactly what the person is afraid of—things like the inability to get/maintain an erection or the inability to have an orgasm. It can cause someone to be so tense that they can't even enjoy the sex, never mind get off on it.

And here, my dear author, is where you have so much room to play.

Let's say your character is so nervous they're struggling to get it up. They're undoubtedly mortified. Now, how does their partner respond? Are they awkward? Angry? Uncertain? Compassionate? Loving? Do they talk their partner through it, or try to physically reassure them? Do they take it personally? This could be a disaster for them and their relationship, or it could be a huge step toward truly trusting each other, or anything in between. With just this single situation—a character unable to maintain an erection due to nerves—there is an *absurd* amount of room for emotional development in the sex scene.

Speaking of performance anxiety, for someone who's nervous, there is little worse than the prospect of one's partner laughing at them in bed. Just thinking about it probably makes a lot of people squirm. So what could be more intimate than being comfortable enough with someone that you can laugh in bed without anyone feeling mocked or degraded? Show your characters being silly in bed. Cracking jokes. Getting so lost in a giggle fit that they pretty much have to start over. Sex doesn't have to be a serious, furtive thing, and some playfulness can go a long way toward demonstrating how comfortable your characters are together. It's also a nice tension breaker for the reader. Gives them a little breather right before the entire plot explodes into chaos.

So those are just some examples of what a sex scene can *do*. We'll touch on that more as we go along.

CHAPTER 2

WHY DOES THIS KEEP HAPPENING?

OR WHY THE HECK DO ALL MY SEX SCENES SOUND THE SAME?

This is a common complaint from both writers and readers. Writers, because they're struggling to keep the scenes from all sounding the same. Readers, because they're tired of reading—and have likely begun skimming—the same scene over and over.

I can relate, because I have experienced both of these. The struggle is real.

But you can fix it!

To start with, here are ways sex scenes can be too similar:

1. **Physical** – characters do the same things in every scene
2. **Emotional** – the emotional impact lessens over time because there's no variation
3. **Vocabulary** – you use the same words/phrases to describe everything
4. **Tone** – every sex scene has the same tone or feeling

Let's start with physical. Are your characters going through the same motions? Using the same positions? Do every scene start with undressing, caressing, some hands, maybe some oral, penetration, and orgasm? Yawn. Mix it up.

Later in this book, I'll go over different practices, such as toys, anal sex, locations besides the bedroom, and group sex. Some of those might provide inspiration for ways your characters could expand their horizons.

If your characters really *do* just want to have sex the same way every time, that's okay too. You can either mix it up emotionally (we'll get to that in more detail in this chapter!), or just fade to black. If the sex needs to be the same as it was in the last scene, then there's really no reason to show it. It'll just lessen the impact of the previous scene and bore your reader. And that is something you absolutely do not want—*a bored reader*.

So for addressing *physical* repetition, I recommend:

- Add some variety
- Lean harder on emotion
- If the scene truly doesn't offer anything different from the last one, don't be afraid to fade to black

Now how about sex scenes that are the same emotionally?

Sit back and think about some of the scenes you've written that seem to echo each other but don't have the same physical mechanics. Are they lacking an emotional punch?

Remember that sex scenes are as versatile emotionally as they are physically. A new couple taking their relationship to the next level, an established couple being intimate and affectionate, makeup sex, hate sex, angry sex, breakup sex, reunion sex—the list goes on.

This is also where the tone can come into play, since that's pretty closely intertwined with emotions. It can be an intense, quiet scene packed with emotions the characters can't quite express verbally. It can be clumsy and frantic because the characters can't wait another second. It can be silly and funny—don't underestimate incorporating humor into sex scenes (there's a whole chapter on that later on)!

A sex scene also doesn't have to involve a massive emotional shift. It can demonstrate the characters bonding, or show that they're drifting apart. It can simply show that your character is more confident than they were a few scenes ago, or more insecure. It can be a tension breaker after a lot of rough non-sex scenes (e.g., taking a breather during an intense thriller). Not every scene is required to mean something profound emotionally or with regard to the relationship.

Finally, vocabulary is an issue that can make sex scenes repetitive. And it's a tough one, because there are only so many ways to describe certain things. It's not uncommon at all for a writer to, in an attempt to change up the vocabulary, write something unintentionally hilarious or gross. As a result, we all end up falling back on the tried and true— avoiding the throbbing members and just using dicks and cocks.

So what do you do?

My approach is to focus less on the actual body parts. If you find yourself trying to come up with eight different ways to say "cock" so you're not repeating it over the course of two paragraphs, that problem is quite likely that you're mentioning cocks eight times in two paragraphs. Instead, zoom out. Focus on feelings. Sensory details. Emotional responses. Sprinkle in some more dialogue. Don't focus so hard on varying the words when the issue is likely that you need to move the camera around a little more.

Unless your characters are doing something highly specific or unusual that needs to be explicitly detailed for the reader to follow along, trust them to make inferences. You don't have so spell out every single bead of sweat or thrust of hips in ultra high def. In fact, you'll probably lose your reader if you do.

So now we've covered a few ways you can add some variety and avoid repetition, but we need to put it into practice! How about an exercise? Yep, folks. This book is interactive. You want to learn to write better sex scenes—you're gonna have to write some sex scenes.

Ready? Pencils UP!

1. Write a sex scene.
2. The specifics aren't important. I'd suggest keeping it relatively short—500-1000 words.
3. Go forth and do so now.
4. Yes, now.
5. Go!
6. Good job!
7. Now write the scene again.
8. *Stick with me here.*
9. Keep the physical mechanics *exactly* the same. Whatever motions they go through in the original, keep them here.
10. But... make it different.
11. Change the emotions. Change the dialogue. Change the sensory details. Change the tone.
12. Just don't change the physical mechanics.

I know, it's challenging, but there's a method to my madness.

Compare your scenes side by side. Yes, they'll still be repetitive. That's okay because this is an exercise. The point is to see how much variation you can create by changing up everything besides the physical.

You can take the *exact same physical scene*, change the tone, emotions, and vocabulary, and turn it into a completely *different experience*.

Because that's really what it comes down to: each scene is an experience, and your readers don't want to relieve the exact same experience over and over again.

With all of this in mind, you should be able to add some variety to your sex scenes, and break out of that pesky pattern of scenes that all sound the same!

To Recap:

- If you find yourself trying to find 8 different ways to say "cock" in 2 paragraphs, the problem *isn't* needing different ways to say "cock."
- Mix up the physical mechanics if it works for your story.
- When in doubt, focus on tone and emotions.
- Don't insult your reader's intelligence.

CHAPTER 3

WHEN TO SHOW, WHEN TO TELL, & WHEN TO FADE TO BLACK

There are a lot of people with a lot of opinions about erotic fiction, even when they don't actually read or write it themselves. I can't even tell you how many hours of my life I've wasted in online arguments with people pushing the snobbish idea that sex scenes should be avoided on principle.

Why do I bother arguing? Not because I expect to change the minds of the people spouting those asinine assertions, but for the benefit of lurkers who might be on the fence. Yeah, it's a lot like a political discussion, and it gets about as heated too.

Amidst all these opinionfests, I've heard it said that if a sex scene has some sort of depth, then there's no reason that depth can't be shown through other scenes (yet no one can explain to me why a sex scene is a less valid means of conveying that depth). I've been told that sex scenes turn books into porn rags. You name it, I've heard it.

As far as I'm concerned, it's all nonsense. Sex is an extremely intimate act, and myriad emotions can be conveyed through that act. Dismissing it entirely as a valid means of human interaction—one that should *never* be expressed in art and *always* be replaced by something arbitrarily deemed superior—is absurd.

At the same time, there *is* a balance to be struck. How much sex is too much, and how much is not enough?

As they say... how long is a piece of rope?

How much sex belongs in the story really depends on the story as well as the tone and pacing. If your book is about a boxer, chances are there are going to be a lot of boxing scenes. If your book is about a relationship growing in part through the sexual content, or the story is about someone's sexual exploration, you'll probably have a lot more sex scenes.

The question is not, "How much sex should I include in a book?"

It's "How much sex will help me tell this story?"

The answer might be zero. It might be two or three scenes strategically placed throughout the book. It might be twenty. As long as your story is moving forward and holding your reader's interest, you're good.

Variety is a great way to keep up pacing and hold a reader's interest. If your book is going along at a nice clip, then there's six sex scenes in a row that aren't much different from one to the next, it's going to kill your pacing. The problem isn't that you have too many sex scenes—it's that you have too many *repetitive* scenes stacked on top of each other, and your story *isn't moving forward*. The same thing would happen if you had half a dozen fight scenes without much variation, or if you (for reasons I can't begin to fathom, since I hate writing car chases) decided to have six car chases one after the other. (that sound you hear is me shuddering at the thought of writing that many car chases in one book)

The point is to focus less on how many sex scenes you

have and more on whether they're serving their intended purpose without hurting your pacing.

Let's say you had a sex scene in chapter 3. Now the characters are in the mood to get freaky in chapter 6, but they're probably going to be doing similar things to what they did before. You can show the whole scene. But should you? If your book is erotic fiction, you might be tempted to write the scene because... this is erotic fiction. Of course you're going to write all the sex.

In fact, I've heard it argued that one should never fade to black in erotic fiction, but like most absolutes, this one is ridiculous. In erotic fiction, a sex scene is *more likely* to be played out on-camera, but they don't *all* have to be played out. Many of them probably shouldn't be. The last thing you want is your reader rolling their eyes and muttering, "Here we go again."

You can avoid this by being mindful of your pacing.

- Does *this* sex scene need to happen on-screen?
- Do I need more action, dialogue, etc., between these sex scenes?
- Is this really the best time for the characters to have sex, or should they be focused on other matters?

If you can't justify the scene's existence... skip it. Fade to black and keep your story rolling.

And don't think of fading to black as a mood killer or a cockblock. Fading to black can be hot in its own right—it can leave the reader imagining what happened after the curtain fell. Letting their imagination run wild, letting them fill in the blanks, can be seriously sexy.

To illustrate this, here's a snippet from *The Husband*

Gambit where Hayden and Jesse are fooling around on their balcony on a cruise.

"You know, at the rate we're going," he murmured, "we'll end up spending this entire cruise naked in our suite." He cupped my ass. "We're going to miss all the excursions."

I rocked my hips just right to rub our dicks together. "You make that sound like a bad thing."

"Mmm, not at all." He kneaded my ass, pulling me against him. "Just saying."

"Well, duly noted." I lifted my head so I could look in his eyes. "For the record, I have no problem with crossing out the itinerary and replacing it with 'annoy the neighbors with loud sex.'"

Jesse laughed. "I did hear the neighbors coming back to their suite when I went to get the corkscrew." He slid his hands up my back. "Think we should go annoy them?"

"Fuck yes we should."

- The Husband Gambit

The scene—and the chapter—ends there. *Could* I have written the subsequent sex scene? Sure. And I was tempted to, because quite honestly, Jesse and Hayden were a lot of fun to write together.

In this case, though, the scene would've slowed the pacing dramatically. The book is fairly light when it comes to on-page sex, and this is only a chapter or two after the first (and so far only) sex scene. In the interest of not slowing down the pacing with a lot of back-to-back sex in a long book that is otherwise minimal in that department, I chose to fade to black here, giving the reader just enough to imagine what happened next. Sometimes that is hotter and more evocative than showing the scene itself.

Alternatively, if you encounter a place where a sex scene would happen but doesn't need to be shown, you can start the scene immediately *after* the act. In this example, the characters have been hooking up throughout the book. The sex scene won't reveal anything new, and it won't be much different from others that have come before it, but this chapter involved them having a conversation in bed.

So, I skipped the sex and opened the chapter like this:

"Oh my God." I dropped onto Parker's rumpled bed, sweating and trembling. "Wow."

He collapsed beside me on his stomach, breathing as hard as I was. "Fuck. Wow is right."

I grinned drunkenly. I'd been here all of ten minutes, and we'd wasted no time getting naked. The second I'd walked through his front door, he'd kissed me, and he'd pleaded against my lips for me to get the hell out of my pants and fuck him.

I had. Dear Lord, I had. It'd been fast and furious, a quickie to end all quickies, but after not seeing him for two weeks, I'd been as eager as he was.

- Cole, *Gentlemen of the Emerald City, book 2*

There's still enough to convey what they did and how

much they enjoyed it, but without a gratuitous scene. No repetition and no lost pacing.

I'm not advocating cutting sex scenes at all costs. Not by any means. These are simply alternatives for places where such a scene would happen, but wouldn't necessarily add to —and might, in fact, slow down—the story. It's the same principle as skipping over conversations that won't reveal anything new ("he filled her in on what the boss had told him") or putting in a scene break instead of showing characters moving from point A to point B. *Any* scene that bogs down your story is worth scrutinizing for a potential visit to the chopping block.

Much like I would advise against cutting sex scenes just because they're sex scenes, I also caution against the opposite extreme—keeping a sex scene just because it's a sex scene. As with any scene—car chases, conversations, cooking scenes—if your reader will be tempted to skim, it's probably not serving any purpose. Skip it.

To recap...

- Determine how much sex is necessary to fully tell your story.
- Cut any scene whose only real function is to slow down your pacing.
- Don't underestimate how sexy it can be to fade to black or pick up after an off-screen sex scene.

CHAPTER 4

DON'T YOU TAKE THAT TONE WITH ME

TONE & VOCABULARY

Words matter, y'all.

One place where sex scenes can go off the rails comes down to the choice of words. Obviously, right? That's what writing is—choosing words.

Except this often becomes a major pitfall with a sex scene. An otherwise gritty and sharply-written thriller reaches a sex scene, and the writing suddenly switches to either Penthouse Forum level smut or flowery prose that shies away from all but the most socially acceptable euphemisms.

Now, there's nothing inherently wrong with any of those styles—they all have their place—but they don't necessarily go *together*. A Caesar salad tastes great and so does chocolate ganache, but you probably wouldn't mix them, right? Same principle, and the shift between tone/styles can be so jarring that the sex scene won't fit at all into the story. As a result, betas and editors—not to mention readers—will declare that the scene was unnecessary and should've been cut.

Yet the problem wasn't the scene itself. It was the way it was written.

It was the words. The tone. The vocabulary. The ganache was perfect—it just didn't belong on the salad.

If your writing style is lyrical, your sex scenes should be lyrical. If your voice is gritty and curse-laden, keep that going when the clothes come off. If the story is light and silly, then why did you suddenly turn sober and serious for the sex scene?

Now, there is absolutely a time and a place for a jarring shift in style. Style, like anything in a story, shouldn't be static. The trick is doing it deliberately and for effect, not because "well, this is a sex scene, so I need to write it like a sex scene."

Don't write it "like a sex scene." Write it *like a scene in your story*. It's a scene just like any other scene. Keep your voice and tone consistent unless you're altering them for a deliberate and specific effect.

When it comes to tone and vocabulary, approach your sex scene with these questions in mind:

- What is the tone of the whole story? (e.g., light, heavy, fluffy, dark)
- Should this scene's tone or voice deviate from the rest of the story or the sex scenes that happen before/after? Why, how, and to what effect?
- What words and phrases fit your character's voice? How would this character describe what's happening?

Character voice is crucial here. Much like the tone of the story shouldn't change just because it's a sex scene, the character's voice should remain consistent, too. Your character who peppers every sentence with "fuck" like it's a punctuation mark isn't going to suddenly shy away from using the cruder euphemisms in the bedroom. Likewise, your extremely conservative character who won't use anything harsher than "darn" isn't going to suddenly channel dialogue from porn. Of course, as with anything, these bedroom 180s can happen—they should just happen because the writer made a conscious choice to reveal something about the character, not because "eh, it's a sex scene, who cares?"

An exceptional example of character voice in sex scenes can be found in L.J. Hayward's *Death and the Devil* series. I hesitate to actually quote the scenes because there's a risk of spoilers—the plots of these books are intricately woven masterclasses in releasing information to the reader in precisely the right dose at exactly the right time. And yes, even a quote from a sex scene could potentially spoil something. What I will say is that the characters, Jack and Ethan, have incredibly different voices right from the start. Jack is crass and crude—not excessively so, he's just got that grizzled former spec ops vibe. Ethan is quite the opposite—he's very reserved and almost prudish in his thoughts and words.

These vibes and voices carry over beautifully into the sex scenes. Where it's not at all out of place for Jack to refer to cocks and cum, it would be woefully out of character for Ethan. It's an exceptional series for a lot of reasons, not the least of which is the voices of both men... including in the sex scenes.

Now, as far as individual words, particularly euphemisms, it's hard to pick words that sound sexy. And really, there are only so many nicknames for body parts, so the last thing you probably want to hear from me is that they get even *more* limited when you're trying to maintain a certain tone.

Fact is, though, the words matter. Your word choice can make your scene silly, sexy, or raunchy—any number of things. Where it gets tricky is maintaining that vibe. As a reader, if you're cruising along nice and sensual, and the writer drops in a word that sounds raunchy or juvenile, it's going to throw off the whole scene. A sensual scene *probably* won't benefit from "cum splattered all over her tits" any more than a more pornographic scene would from a "throbbing manhood" or a "molten core."

Think about these euphemisms for penis:

Cock. Shlong. Member. Manhood. Dick. Wang. Weiner. Erection.

They're all naming the same body part, but they're *not* interchangeable. Each word describes the exact same thing, just to varying degrees of crudeness and palatability. They each bring their own implications about tone and voice, ranging from flowery to something you would literally expect from Beavis & Butthead, and I don't have to spell out which is which.

Another example: Semen.

Jizz. Spooge. Emission. Cum. Seed.

Vagina euphemisms are, in my opinion, the toughest. There aren't very many, and there are even fewer that work well (again in my opinion) in a sex scene.

Can you use "cunt"?

Yes. You can use any word you want. Be aware, however, of the visceral reaction some readers will likely have to it. It's extraordinarily offensive to most Americans, but it's practically a term of endearment in other places.

So in general, which word(s)/tone *should* you choose? Depends on your story. I've written plenty of stories where "dick" or "cock" were the best choices. In others, even something as benign as "erection" was pushing the envelope.

Like anything, it can change within the same book, too. The shift can occur in one character—say, one who starts out shy about sex, but comes into their own as the story goes on. Their vocabulary will likely evolve as well, becoming more direct and graphic, even if they don't necessarily adopt the more vulgar euphemisms. L.J. Hayward's *Death and the Devil* series is, again, an excellent example of this evolution.

As with most things in this book—and indeed with writing in general—it comes down to what works best in the story you're writing. You can do anything, but do it deliberately, mindfully, and for effect.

And finally, the issue of a somewhat limited vocabulary brings with it another problem: repetition. It's incredibly easy to find yourself either using a specific word—cock, for example—so many times it's hilariously conspicuous, or trying so hard to find other words to avoid repetition that you end up coming up with bizarre similes and metaphors.

If you realize you're in either of these situations... stop.

Step back.

Is the problem that you're not changing up the words enough?

Or is the real issue that you're focusing too much on body parts? As I mentioned in a previous chapter, the problem most likely isn't that you need eight different ways to refer to a penis in two paragraphs—it's that you've referred to a penis too many times. Oftentimes, especially in sex scenes, the solution to repetition isn't using a different euphemism—it's focusing on different things. Emotions. Sensations. Reactions. Dialogue. Those will often do far more to avoid repetition, and make your scene a more engaging read.

To recap:

- Know thy voice.
- Know thy character's voice.
- Shifts in either should be deliberate and for effect, not just because you're now writing a sex scene.
- Be mindful of euphemisms and the effect they have on your tone and voice.
- Emotions and sensations over body parts.
- You really should read L.J. Hayward's *Death and the Devil* series.

CHAPTER 5

MOVIES ARE YOUR FRIEND

One way to amp up your sex scenes is to spend some time watching how sex scenes are filmed. I'm not talking about porn—I'm talking about the movies they show at the theater. Hollywood. Indie films. Possibly Bollywood, but as I've only seen a handful of Bollywood films, I won't pretend to be any kind of authority on their content, erotic or otherwise.

Our society—particularly American society—is a strange mix of oversexualized and puritanically prudish. Sex is everywhere, but it's often ensconced in metaphor, which can actually make it exponentially hotter. Because of censorship laws and movie ratings, filmmakers have to get extra creative in order to convey sexuality. Ironically they don't have to get quite as creative about conveying violence, but that's a different book.

Anyway. Sex scenes in movies can run the gamut of "kissing passionately, then cut to waking up naked" to "one stray camera angle away from a porno." There are limits to what can be shown, though. Indie films can generally get away with a lot more, and there have been a number of films over the years where the actors actually had sex in order to create the scene, but for the most part, the activities are more implied than shown. In order to keep a film from the dreaded NC-17 rating[1], filmmakers can typically get away with naked butts and breasts, but things get sketchy when full frontal nudity is involved. Once hands and mouths start drifting over those areas, particularly without the buffer of clothes, the censors and critics start losing their minds. And you definitely won't see any penetration.

As such, sex scenes in film are accomplished through a whole lot of implication. If a character is on top of another character, and they're both obviously naked aside from the sheet covering them from the waist down, and they're kissing and/or moving their hips in a thrusting motion... we don't need to actually see the penetration shot to know they're having sex. If one character is kissing the other's neck, then continues to move downward and ultimately out of the frame, but the remaining character's facial expression shows increasing amounts of surprise, pleasure, or what have you... it doesn't take Sherlock Holmes to figure out there's some oral sex going on.

Of course, when we're writing erotic scenes, we're not limited the way Hollywood is. If we're so inclined and the story calls for it, we can get down to the finer details that would condemn a film to the NC-17 black hole. That said, I think it's worthwhile for an author to spend some time observing how filmmakers convey their erotic scenes while still toeing the line of quote-unquote *decency*.

First, grab a piece of paper and make a list of five or ten sex scenes that have stuck with you from TV or movies. Now go over your list and ask yourself why those scenes were so memorable. If it's "because I saw Susie Stardust's nipple" or "because I saw Max Actorpants's pubes," keep thinking.

- Did the scene leave you feeling turned on?
- Did it make you uncomfortable?
- Was it heartbreaking?
- Was it sensual?

If you need to, look up the scene on YouTube and watch it again. Besides nipples or pubes, what makes that scene stand out in your mind?

I won't tell you what your answers are or should be because we all take different things from different scenes. There are no wrong answers here. It's worth considering your answers, though, because they just might give you some insight into how to make your reader feel that way when reading your scenes.

With all of that in mind, I'm going to touch on some specific scenes and why I think they're valuable for writers. We'll start with *Titanic*. I'm going to assume you've seen it, but if not, go online and look up these two scenes:

1. The scene where Jack is drawing Rose.
2. The backseat scene.

When Jack is drawing Rose, we see her lying on a couch, naked except for the gigantic diamond. At one point, when Jack is shading the contour of Rose's breast, he blushes, which she teases him about. In the present, elderly Rose mentions it was the most erotic experience of her life, and I would argue it's one of the most erotic moments in the movie. Not the actual shot of her naked breast, but of Jack shading it with his finger—whether the director intended it or not, this can absolutely be a metaphor for Jack physically touching Rose. Though they never physically touch in that scene, it's every bit as sensual as if they'd had sex right there on the couch. Quite possibly more so, given the tension thrumming between them.

Not long after, they find themselves in the backseat of a car in the cargo hold. We see them kiss, and we see her put his hand on her clothed breast. Cue more heated kissing, and then we're outside the car, where we see fogged up windows and the famous Hand—Rose's hand smacking the window before sliding down. Then we return to the interior with the naked, sweaty pair who have obviously just had sex.

We don't actually witness the act, but we know they weren't playing Monopoly in there. I would argue that the backseat scene falls into the gray area between an explicit sex scene and a fade-to-black. We don't see the parts that would have turned Titanic into a porno, but in between the fade-out (fully-clothed kissing) and the fade-in (naked and out of breath), we have the hand on the window. All the passion and eroticism of a fully drawn sex scene are condensed into seconds of a hand hitting and sliding down fogged-up glass.

This isn't to argue that sex scenes should be as condensed as possible. Not at all. What I'm pointing out here is how much can be conveyed without focusing the camera lens on the tab-A slot-B part of the action.

In essence, because of everything the camera has to *avoid*—the body parts and activities that would result in an NC-17 rating—the filmmakers eroticize everything *else* in order to successfully create their scene. We as writers don't have to shy away from the forbidden parts, but because of this, it's easy to then overlook all the things filmmakers have to rely on. The very things that can make a scene a million times sexier than an extreme close-up of penetration.

There's a scene in *Meet Joe Black* where the title character has sex for the first time ever. It's a beautiful scene, and for most of the "action"—where they're quite obviously having intercourse—we don't see more than the characters' faces. Little more than their eyes, really. There's telltale movement, and the characters are obviously naked, but the story is told in their facial expressions.

Toward the beginning of 300, there's an unusual sex scene between King Leonidas and Queen Gorgo. Like the rest of the movie, it's highly stylized with super slow motion that's almost still in places. The lighting, interestingly enough, is entirely cool—very dark with lots of blues and grays. There's some music, but the soundtrack is mostly the actress's gasps and heavy breathing even though it's clear the actor is quite vocal as well. Little is left to the imagination about what they're doing, but the filmmaker's choices when it comes to light and shadow, sound and silence, shown and implied, make what could have been a generic sex scene into something much more erotic. Also, even when only one character's face is visible, the focus on each other is undeniable.

And of course, let's not forget the famous library scene in *Atonement*. There's a conspicuous absence of music, which lets the viewer hear the characters and their movements, and there's also an absence of bare skin. Robbie is dressed in a tux, and though it's clear they undo his pants, he doesn't undress. Cecilia's green dress covers everything except her back and neck, but there are two particularly erotic moments involving the dress—when Robbie's hand slides over her bare back with the loose spaghetti strap between his fingers, and when the skirt is pulled up to bare her thigh. As with the other scenes I've described, it's obvious the characters are having sex—albeit in a not terribly comfortable position—but everything is either implied or shown through responses and facial expressions.

Another worthwhile scene for a writer to watch is the sex scene in *Enemy at the Gate*. The characters have to be completely quiet because they're in a room full of sleeping soldiers, and their facial expressions and sharp movements don't let you forget a) how badly they want each other, b) how intense the sex is, and c) how much they're struggling to stay quiet.

Finally, stepping away from films for a moment, there's a music video that's an absolutely exquisite example of erotic—*The Father Project* by Norwegian artist Tooji. The first half of the video builds up the tension between the characters, and when they finally connect, it's spectacularly hot. From there, the characters are obviously having sex—they're fully nude and out in the open—but most of the sensuality is conveyed through hands on skin. All through the video, there are shots of hands running over bare skin, and I would argue those are just as hot as the shots of one character riding the other.

With Tooji's permission, I adapted *The Father Project* into a short story, *Just Hear Me*, and this is how the kiss from the music video played out on the page:

Jordan didn't move. He should have, and he knew it, but he planted his feet.

They stared at each other. Neither spoke. Neither moved.

God, please...

Tell me...

Without a word, eyes locked on Jordan's, Darius closed some of the distance between them, and

Jordan held his breath as Darius slowly—slowly—lifted his hand and reached for him.

What do I...

Soft fingertips brushed Jordan's cheek. The other hand went to the back of his neck.

The sliver of space between them was shrinking, the high-walled sanctuary around them fading, and—

Forgive me, Lord, for wanting this so much.

—Darius kissed him.

And the world didn't stop.

It started moving again. It was like everything had been in suspended animation since he'd walked out of Darius's apartment, and now it wasn't. The world was spinning. His heart was beating. He could breathe.

- Just Hear Me

That moment is only a few fleeting seconds onscreen, but you can see how much emotional and physical subtext can be pulled from something that happens so fast.

The scenes I described above are just a few examples of memorably erotic sex scenes on film, and I don't even get into the scenes of foreplay, or the moments characters make connections. Smoldering eye contact. Suggestive touches. The loaded hesitation before a decisive kiss. Watch these, and watch them closely, and translate that crackling tension and barely contained desire to the page.

As a writer instead of a filmmaker, remember that you have both advantages and disadvantages. Unlike the filmmaker, you can tap into other senses—showing us what a character feels, tastes, and smells as well as hearing and seeing. You can show us the character's internal thoughts. Conversely, you don't have the luxury of putting the image in front of the reader's eyeballs. You have to use words to convey all the senses and thoughts and actions. But hey, you're a writer. That's what you do! You've got this.

One final thought along these lines—you can use words to convey the senses and thoughts of your POV character, but what about their partner? If you're writing in first or in third limited, you've got to rely on your character's interpretations of the signals their partner is sending. This is another place where watching sex scenes can come in handy—watch one of the characters and pay close attention to their body language. How would a partner read those signals? How would they make the partner feel? What would they do to either get more of those signals (if it's something positive) or fewer (if it's something negative). Remember, sex is a feedback loop of sorts—stimulus, response, stimulus, response—and unless your character is a telepath, they'll have to rely on physical and visual cues. Film is a good resource for this, and amateur[2] porn is too, though I'll address that more in the next chapter.

When you're writing a sex scene or the scene(s) leading up to one, think about the things filmmakers use to tell you what's happening. Not just the thrusty parts, but how the characters are feeling.

How does a filmmaker convey that a sex scene is sensual? Desperate? Playful? Aggressive?

How do we know characters are enjoying themselves?

How can we tell the moment of penetration or when a character is climaxing?

Think about what's going through the character's mind in a particular moment. Is their stomach fluttering? Is their heart racing? Can they breathe? What happens when they get close enough to feel the other person's body heat, or smell their scent, or brush clothes against clothes or skin against skin? Watch their responses closely, and put those into your scene.

Exercise:

- **Look at your list of sex scenes from earlier, and pull one up on YouTube.** Watch the scene, then write it. Pay close attention to the sensations, feelings, and actions in the scene, and focus on bringing those to life on the page. Does your scene have the same vibe as the one you watched? Do the same emotions and sensations come through? (You can also do this as a buddy exercise and swap with a beta reader for their feedback.)

- **Repeat the above exercise using a scene from a show or movie you *haven't* seen before.** (Do a search for "love scene" or "sex scene" and browse until you find one from a film/show you haven't seen) The purpose of this is to write it without any context or knowledge of the characters outside of the sex scene. You're not going for canon here; the purpose of the exercise is to learn how the filmmaker conveyed sensations, feelings, and actions, and to translate those onto the page.

- **Write one of the scenes above, but change something.** If it's a playful scene, make it intensely emotional. If it's reunion sex, make it breakup sex. If the characters are good at it, make them awkward. Pay close attention to what you change in order to convey that new dynamic.

To Recap:

- Pay attention to the things filmmakers rely on to convey what they can't show directly.
- Don't lose sight of those things because you can show what they can't.

CHAPTER 6

BOW-CHICKA-THAT DOESN'T LOOK FUN

LET'S TALK ABOUT PORN.

Upfront, I'll state that I'm aware that the porn industry is messy, rife with abuse, and not at all above exploiting participants. I've worked in the industry myself, though fortunately for a company that was scrupulous about remaining above board both legally and ethically.

As with many things, entire books could (and should) be written on the darker aspects of the adult industry, if ethical consumption of porn is possible, etc. This is, of course, beyond the scope of this book.

In this chapter, I am making no moral judgments on those who consume porn, but rather pointing out—from the perspective of an erotic fiction writer—that one should be aware of what is realistic, what translates poorly from the filmed scene to the written one, etc.

So with that addressed, let's talk about using porn for research. Don't laugh—many, *many* writers have perused porn in the name of both research and inspiration. It can be a good way to see if a particular position is physically possible, for example.

But take what you see in porn with a grain of salt.

I say this from experience, too—for a brief period in the late 1990s, I edited pornos, and the finished product is very, very different from the real thing. I'm not talking about the setups and "stories." No one watches porn for the plot, y'all —I don't need to tell you that your car breaking down in the middle of the desert probably won't lead to an interlude with a shirtless dude with a six-pack while cheesy music plays in the background. Or maybe I just broke down in the wrong desert. I don't know.

The part I want to address in this chapter is how sex differs between porn and reality. Hollywood lies to you about how guns, relationships, and natural disasters work, and porn lies to you about how sex works.

There's a lot you don't see in a finished porno. Not just the airbrushing, makeup, industrial grade hair removal, and the simultaneous absence of certain bodily fluids and some-what alarming *over*abundance of *others*. When you see a twenty-minute video, it's quite likely the editor had at least an hour of footage to work with, and that's if the crew only used one camera. On sets with bigger budgets, you'll likely have multiple cameras, and the shoots will go on for hours. Plural.

From this footage, the editors cut out the fumbles, the leg cramps, the people needing a minute to catch their breath, and the less-than-graceful position changes. They salvage the most flattering shots and stitch them together to create a finished product, and yes, they absolutely reuse clips to extend the scene if they're short on usable video. It's almost magic what someone can make out of a handful of good segments. In fact, you would be amazed how generous some creative editing can be for a penis that really, *really* doesn't want to stay hard.

The point here is that, to say the least, porn takes a *lot* of liberty with reality.

But when we're talking about the live action stuff, there *are* real human bodies involved, which means there *is* a certain amount of reality in a porno. Double penetration couldn't happen in a porno if it wasn't physically possible. The exotic and acrobatic positions might take some work, but they *can* clearly be done, even if they aren't super comfortable or they require someone to be double-jointed. And as we've been shown time and time again, yes it is possible for a cock that big to fit that far down someone's throat.

So if you're looking to see if a scene/act you have in mind is doable, porn is a reasonable resource... to a point.

The thing to remember is that porn is *for the cameras*. Many of the positions the actors use are done because they look hot, not because they're fun or even comfortable.

For example, there's a variation of reverse cowgirl that's used so often, I almost wonder if it's been made mandatory by the High Council of Pornography[1]. The guy is usually sitting back in a chair, and the woman turns so her back is to him, then straddles him. In order to get the best penetration shot, the actors are tilted and contorted in ways that must be absolutely excruciating after a while. Especially when you consider how long it actually takes to film something like that, not to mention the enormous high heels she's probably wearing.

Point being, positions like that are meant for the *camera*, not the *participants*.

If you move such a position into an erotic scene, you run the danger of losing your reader.

"That... doesn't sound comfortable."

"Oh man, does she want to dislocate her hip? Because that's how you dislocate a hip."

"My neck hurts just reading this..."

For this reason, my suggestion is if you really want to use porn as a form of research, err on the side of amateur porn. Like, real amateur porn—the kind where two people set up a camera in their bedroom and go at it for a while. The professionally produced amateur porn is more realistic than the pro-acted stuff, but even they use a certain amount of Hollywood magic—camera angles, the occasional instruction from the director, and editing.

Professionally produced or not, you usually can't go wrong with videos that feature amateurs, if only because they're not going to contort themselves quite the way the pros do. They'll show signs of fatigue. Erections may flag from time to time (such as while bottoming, or just because the person is tired). People will sweat. The more acrobatic positions won't last quite as long. Emissions won't be quite as... copious.

In short, while there is still an element of performance for the cameras, you're generally going to find more realistic acts and positions between amateurs than professionals.

To recap:

- Porn is an ethical minefield.
- What you see in porn is done for the cameras, not the pleasure of the participants.
- Amateurs have the edge on realism over professionals.

CHAPTER 7

DID YOU SEE/HEAR/SMELL/TASTE/FEEL THAT?

WRITING THE SENSES

If you want to engage your reader fully, you need to engage their senses. Don't just tell them about the moving parts and the squishy bits. Ideally, you want to create a scene so vivid the reader can't help but feel what the character feels—physically *and* emotionally.

So, let's talk about senses. Of course there's the big five...

- Taste
- Touch
- Smell
- Sound
- Sight

There's some dispute on how many senses we actually have, though. I've seen numbers all over the board, with the upper end being around twenty-one to over fifty. These can include perception of balance, hot and cold, movement, body position (e.g., where your limbs are in relation to each other and objects around you), and pain.

How many should you include in a given scene? As

many as it takes to create the vivid sensory picture you want to create.

One area where I see new writers struggle sometimes is focusing so hard on the big picture, the miss the little details. And the little details are often what sticks with the readers. This is something to think about when you get to the chapter on movies and television: notice how often the camera will zoom in on small things. Lips or fingertips drifting over skin are a favorite. I've even seen tight shots on an area of skin as a goose bumps spring to life.

Basically, don't concentrate so hard on thrusting hips that you overlook fingers digging into shoulders or sweat sliding over skin. Don't just tell us what they look like— show us what they *feel* like. Show us the cool sensation of air touching the damp skin their partner just kissed. Show us the sensory chain reaction of one sense triggering others:

> The heady sweetness of her pussy seemed to sober me up and intoxicate me at the same time—kicking the tequila right out of the picture and giving me an entirely new reason to be dizzy and halfway out of my mind.

- Stuck Landing

While we're at it, read the above snippet again, this time paying close attention to whether the character says "I tasted..." or "I felt..."

She doesn't, does she? This is not by accident—it's a conscious choice to avoid filtering.

What is filtering? Simply put:

- Filtering: I saw him walk away.
- No filtering: He walked away.

Filtering is not incorrect. There's nothing wrong with it. However, it does create a small degree of separation between the reader and the sensation. If what you're looking for is more immediate and immersive sensory writing, consider removing filters as much as possible.

Similarly, if you want to *create* some distance, filters can work to your advantage. For example, if you have a character who is deep in subspace or otherwise not firmly anchored in the present, the added distance can emphasize that effect:

He heard his Dom's voice from a million miles away.

This is most effective if you've used filtering sparingly. If all the other sensory details have been immediate and unfiltered, the one above will have more distinct distance.

As I mentioned in the chapter on repetition, sensory writing can also help add variety. You could theoretically write your characters going through the exact same physical motions in every scene, but change them up dramatically through sensory details and emotional responses. (I don't recommend actually *doing* that—just emphasizing how important those details are and how much of an impact they have.)

This is also a way to convey the intimacy of the moment. A scene that focuses more heavily on physical details will contrast dramatically with a scene that's more tuned in to emotional responses. Neither is superior to the other—they simply serve different purposes. If your book is a romance where your characters start out as casual lovers, for example, the sex early on might have a more physical feel while the later scenes—those after the characters have a deeper bond—will feel more emotionally intimate.

You can use sensory details for both of these things.

To illustrate this, here are clips from the first and last sex scenes of the same book. In the first, Ethan has hired Luca, an escort, for sex.

I moaned and kissed him again, and I wasn't in any hurry either. Not when I had this beautiful naked man under me, his skin hot against mine as we kissed and he stroked me. I shifted onto one arm so I could return the favor, and... ungh. *Jesus.* I'd known for a long time that I needed this, but I'd had no idea how much I needed it until I was absolutely drowning in sex with the most beautiful man I'd ever seen.

- Luca, Gentlemen of the Emerald City Book 1

Later, their relationship has evolved, so the sex feels—and reads—differently too:

Rocking his hips slowly, Ethan raked his eyes all over me. He stared down for a long moment, lips moving in soundless curses as he watched himself fucking me, and then he slid his gaze all the way up to my face. My breath caught. It wasn't the first time he'd looked at me like that—all hunger and love and need—but I'd been absolutely convinced he'd never look at me that way again.

I reached for him, and he came down to me, and the touch of his lips to mine sent electricity crackling through every nerve in my body. Having him over me, against me, inside me, and kissing me —it was literally impossible to get closer to him, and I loved every second of it.

- Luca, Gentlemen of the Emerald City Book 1

While we're on the subject of describing what a character is feeling physically, I've had some editors object to phrases like "his heart pounded in his chest." The response is... well, where *else* would it be pounding? His ears, for one, but I digress. To me, this is one of those areas where it's less about being specific—assuming this isn't science fiction, the reader doesn't need to be told where the heart is located—and more about creating a vivid feeling that the reader can relate to. It's much the same as "his heart pounded against his ribs" or, more to the point, "blood pounded in his ears."

Do you have to specify "in his chest" or anything? No. I'm only mentioning the issue here because I'm very firmly on Team The Reader Isn't Stupid And The Phrase Paints a More Vivid Picture.

This segues into another sensory-adjacent area: independently-moving or autonomous body parts.

Here, too, I am a member of Team The Reader Isn't Stupid, with the substantial caveat that sometimes the wording does paint an odd picture of disembodied limbs taking charge, and indeed, I would recommend changing it.

For example:

- His hand turned the doorknob.

- He turned the doorknob.

He should be running the show here, not his hand. The second option is your better bet.

There are times, though, when what some editors would call autonomous body parts actually work quite nicely, and at least in my experience, some sex scenes can fall into this category. Much like filtering can create some distance between the reader and the sense, this practice can pull the focus in very tight on a particular sensation.

For example:

The brush of fingertips down her spine brought goose bumps to life from her head to her curling toes.

There are editors who would flag both the brushing fingertips and the curling toes as autonomous body parts. And technically, yes, they are, though the toe-curling could arguably be a somewhat involuntary reaction. In this case, though, at least in my opinion, they work. They create a vivid sensory experience, and I firmly believe readers are smart enough not to think it means Thing from The Addams Family is walking up the character's back or that the toes are possessed by demons.

Well, unless of course that's the scene you've set, in which case, mission accomplished.

To recap...

- Use as many senses as you need to make your reader feel what you want them to feel.
- Humans have more than five senses, and many of those can come into play in sex scenes.
- Filtering creates distance.
- Autonomous body parts are subjective.

CHAPTER 8

HE SAID WHAT?

DIALOGUE IN SEX SCENES

I covered a lot of this in the chapter about tone and vocabulary, but this is a bit of a deeper dive. Instead of just focusing on what the characters are thinking and feeling, we're getting into what they might or might not be saying out loud.

To start with, there's a myth that people—especially men—lose the ability to speak during sex. Not that they're speechless or breathless or overwhelmed, but that they literally lose touch with the part of their brain that controls speech.

Can this happen? Can perfectly articulate people be reduced to monosyllabic responses during sex? Sure. But—and I'm sure you've noticed this pattern in this book—it should be done deliberately and with purpose, not just because "eh, anyone with a penis turns into the exact same caveman once said penis gets hard."

The brain definitely gets distracted, but it doesn't shut off entirely. Even at the peak of arousal, your character is still, at their core, the same person they were at the beginning of the scene. Less inhibited, perhaps. Less focused on anything outside their immediate surroundings, sure. But they're coming into the scene with all their personality quirks, past experiences, fears, desires, and emotions, and they'll still have those when the scene is over. Their interactions within that scene will, to varying degrees, be influenced by those things.

And that includes their dialogue.

Dirty talk is tough, y'all. It really is. In fact, it's a little like dialogue in fight scenes—there's a *razor* fine line between saying the right things and resorting to the absolute *cheesefest* that people come up with onscreen. If your dialogue sounds like canned catchphrases that would be mechanically delivered by a porn star or an action star...

I mean, if that's what you're going for, cool. But if it's not, get thee back to the drawing board, and let's get your people talking like, you know, people.

Specifically, let's get them talking like themselves. If you've got a character who never curses, and they're suddenly swearing like a Sailor, it can either be sexy or jarring. It can be comical—a character who's trying desperately to talk dirty, but failing miserably, which has both characters laughing. The same can be awkward, embarrassing, mood-killing; just depends on your characters and your story. It depends on what effect you want from the scene and the interaction. Know your intention, and write for that effect.

Okay, so what should someone actually say when they're talking dirty? Where is that line between the right thing and the cheesefest?

As with everything, it depends. It is incredibly easy to make dirty talk sound awful, but with a deft hand and in the right context, it can be incredibly sexy. In a sensual love-making scene, it might not quite fit, but don't underestimate it in its time and place.

For example, here is a clip from a kink scene between a Dom and a new submissive. The dirty talk is part of how he asserts his dominance.

He stared into Tom's eyes. "If you need me to stop, slap me twice on the thigh. Otherwise, I'm going to fuck you without any mercy at all."

Tom's groan was honey. "Okay."

Consent given, Max loomed over Tom and tightened his grip. "Better fucking open that mouth for me."

That made Tom's eyes widen, but he didn't obey, so Max gripped his hair tight and forced his head back, mindful of his neck. Tom yelped and danced in his chair, then finally opened his mouth wide.

Max straddled Tom's legs and Tom bent forward, giving Max a workable angle.

"That's better." He let go of Tom's chin, and slapped his cock against the side of Tom's mouth. "You have the prettiest lips. I've been wanting to see them stretched around my dick. Better be worth it, or I'm going to upend you and make you pay." He shoved his dick into Tom's waiting mouth.

There was a touch of fear in Tom's groan, but he didn't tap out. He gripped Max's legs, and he worked to both breathe and obey.

That sight, Tom's lips stretched wide, was as gloriously decadent as Max had thought. Wasn't hard to let go, grip Tom's hair in his fist, and start thrusting, pressing in as deep as he could before Tom started to panic.

"You need to do better, Tom," Max growled, and fucked his face harder.

Tears welled in Tom's eyes, but also a fierceness Max hadn't seen before. Tom shuddered and fought back. He didn't struggle, didn't push Max away. Instead, Tom sucked and licked and opened himself to Max.

"Fuck." Max was going to lose his mind. He caught himself on the back of the chair, and gave Tom everything he'd asked for—a rough, brutal face fucking.

Tom relished meeting Max's thrusts, sucking and mouthing Max's cock like it was the only thing that existed in Tom's world, as if he'd been born to pleasure Max.

Max wasn't going to last. Blow jobs usually didn't get him off that hard, but seeing Tom's mouth full of his cock, hearing and feeling the whimpers, watching the tears slide down Tom's cheeks, even as his eyes were pits of fire...it was too much.

He yanked Tom's hair. "You like that, don't you? My fat cock in your throat?"

Tom moaned, and the vibrations nearly undid Max. "Bet you want to suck my come out, eh? Drink it down? Greedy, horny thing that you are." He quickened his thrusts.

- Cinnamon Roll
Anna Zabo

Another point with this scene is that Max is in a particular persona where that kind of talking works. By day, he's a university professor—a linguistics professor, ironically—but in this scene, he's in the role of a Dominant. Specifically, a sadist. While it wouldn't make sense for him to speak this way in his day to day life, dialogue like you see above works when he's playing this particular role.

By contrast, in *Extra Whip*, my characters have a very different dynamic than Max and Tom. While Will and Aaron have a Dom/sub relationship, Will is decidedly much less sadistic than Max, and this comes through in how he speaks to Aaron during a scene:

"You've got me all turned on," I mumbled against his lips. "Kind of feels like you should do something about that."

"Uh-huh. Please." His voice was strained and pleading, just the way I liked it.

Without another word, I let go of his collar and shoved him down onto his knees. As I pushed my dick into his eager mouth, he groaned with pleasure. No one sucked cock like Aaron, especially when he was thanking me for letting him come. He was greedy and hungry, moaning around the head and the shaft as he pumped me with his hand.

"You want more?" I teased.

He moaned, looking up at me with eyes full of need.

Steadying myself with a hand on the bedpost, I rocked my hips, slowly at first, then faster, thrusting into his mouth just like he'd been thrusting into my ass a moment ago.

I gripped his hair tight to make his scalp burn just the way he liked it, and I forced myself into his mouth the same way he'd been forcing himself into my ass—hard, fast, relentless. Like always, he kept a hand firmly on my hip. I was never comfortable forcibly fucking his face unless we both knew he could push me away if he wanted to. He never had, but it was like a safety release on a set of handcuffs —knowing it was there meant we could both lose ourselves without worrying.

"That's it, baby," I growled as he took me closer to the brink. He was so damn good at this—he'd been amazing the very first time he'd gone down on me, and he'd only improved his technique over time. After twenty years...holy fuck.

"God yeah," I breathed. "You're so good at that. Yeah, that's right."

He moaned around my dick as his fingers twitched on my hip.

I thrust as hard as I knew he could handle it— and liked it—as my orgasm closed in. "Mmm, yeah. Perfect. I'm gonna come. You ready for me?"

- Extra Whip

The dialogue here is still dirty, still absolutely sexual, and still with the Dom/sub dynamic firmly in place, but the tone and the words fit *my* characters. The same exchange would be a little too soft for Max and Tom, while Max's words in Will's mouth would come across as wildly out of character. And these are characters within the same series—

characters who know each other—engaging in essentially the same act.

Find your characters' voice and vibe. Don't have them talk the way a Dom should, or the way a virgin should. Have them talk the way *they* should. Be true to your characters' voices, and the rest will fall into place.

To recap:

- One character's perfect dialogue is another's cheesefest.
- People can still communicate verbally during sex.

CHAPTER 9

EDITING & PUBLISHING
& EDITING SOME MORE

To be honest, I could devote an entire book to the intricacies of both editing and publishing erotic fiction. Maybe someday I will, but not here.

I would be remiss, however, if I didn't at least touch on the subject. Between writing your story and having it out there for the world to see, you'll need to edit it and publish it. If you submit it to a publisher, there will be more editing between submission and publication. If you self-publish, don't skimp on the editing either!

So, let's talk about publishers and editors.

The cold hard truth is that when it comes to fiction, most things are subjective. This includes sex. And this extends into the realms of editing and publishing. Trust me when I say there will be moments when you're having a completely serious and professional conversation with your editor about a sex scene, and you'll start giggling like a third grader because... you're having a completely serious and professional conversation with your editor about a sex scene, and it feels kind of ridiculous. Just go with it—you're not the only one.

The point here is that erotic fiction can make edits and publication a little more complicated. You need a publisher (if you plan to go that route) who is willing to confidently stand behind and promote your book. You need an editor who is willing to edit the entire book, not just skim through the sex because it makes them blush (yes, I've had that happen).

Let's start with publishers.

First, publishers are no longer the gatekeepers they once were. Self-publishing is a very viable route—you're reading a self-published book right now! Either route is perfectly valid, and both have their own pros and cons. Here is an incomplete list:

Self-Publishing

- **PROS**:
- Full creative control.
- Retain all rights (including audio and translation, which are both flourishing markets for erotic fiction)
- Ability to make changes if something isn't working (e.g., changing cover art if the one you have isn't selling the book, adjusting prices, expanding to different platforms, etc.)
- **CONS**:
- Can be expensive (edits, cover art, formatting, printing costs, etc.)
- Marketing is 100% your responsibility.
- Difficult to get books into brick-and-mortar bookstores.
- No guarantee of sales or royalties.

Traditional Publishing

- **PROS**
  - No overhead (money flows toward the writer – the publisher pays you, not the other way around!)
  - Professional marketing, editing, artwork, etc.
  - More exposure to wider markets (brick-and-mortar bookstores, etc.).
  - Publishers are motivated to get their investment back, so (in theory) they are motivated to market your book.
- **CONS**
  - Lower royalty percentages.
  - Publisher has final say on edits, art, prices, distribution, etc.
  - You may be locked in for many years, if not the life of your copyright (70 years after you die).
  - May require a literary agent to access.
  - Not all books or authors are promoted equally.

This is nowhere near a complete list for either, and not all publishers are alike. Again, I could write an entire book on the subject. Just make sure you do your due diligence into the market you wish to enter and any company you wish to work with. Talk to other authors. See if there's any scuttlebutt about late/incorrect/stolen royalties, shoddy/problematic editing, or other red flags.

I would caution very strongly against pay-to-play publishers, also known as vanity publishers. They are not in the market of selling books to readers. They're in the market of selling books to authors. If a publisher has "packages" that you pay for in order for them to publish your book, it's very likely a scam. If not a scam, it's something that will benefit the publisher far, far more than it does the author. They have no motivation to market your book because they've already made money off it.

It's up to you which route you want to go. Just do your homework and remember the advice I wish I'd heeded early in my career:

**'Tis better to not be published at all
than it is to be badly published.**

And while we're on the subject of things I learned the hard way so you don't have to:

If you're offered a contract, have an attorney or literary agent look it over for you before you sign. *Trust me.*

Okay. So let's say you do want to go with a publisher, and you've already done your homework and made a list of publishers you're interested in working with.

Now it's time to do a deeper dive and look into their submission guidelines. This is super important anyway. If the publisher requires submissions to be double-spaced Comic Sans in purple font on red paper, then you'd darn well better send your manuscript in double-spaced Comic Sans in purple font on red paper. Those guidelines exist for a reason, and one of those reasons is to weed out writers who don't think guidelines apply to them.

Guidelines can and often do apply to erotic content as well. I've seen publishers who prohibit anything beyond kissing. For those who *will* publish sex, many have limitations about how it appears on-page. Their taboos may come down to legalities and platform terms of service, as there are jurisdictions and platforms that forbid underage characters in erotic content, incest (including pseudoincest), bestiality, etc. Others may just come down to what the specific publishers want in their catalogue for reasons that can range from personal preference to aiming for a specific audience. They may forbid BDSM, or they may only publish BDSM. They may want to stick with books that have a small number of sex scenes, or they may want erotica.

Sometimes it's frustrating to see these limitations, especially if you're struggling to find a home for a particular book. It can be especially frustrating if the guidelines feel judgy, such as when publishers of sweet romances say they want "clean" books. This can be frustrating because of the implications that the opposite is *un*clean, and that sex is dirty, etc. And of course, there are those that include LGBTQ+ content under taboo, regardless of sexual content, which is a whole can of worms in itself.

At the end of the day, it is their prerogative as a publisher to decide what they do and do not accept. While I certainly encourage writers to openly discuss publishers with problematic requirements, I would caution against submitting your work to them out of protest or to try to convince them your book is worth publishing despite its deviation from their guidelines.

I say this for a few reasons.

First and foremost, you're just setting yourself up for disappointment. They're not going to make an exception for your story. As soon as they publish one story that violates their own guidelines, they're opening themselves up for more submissions of the same. They've already made the decision to reject that element, which means they've already made the decision to reject your story before you've taken the time to send it. So don't waste your time or theirs.

Related to this, you really don't want a publisher who is grudgingly accepting your story. If they've put a guideline into place stating they don't want something, and by some stroke of luck, they decide to buy yours... that element they didn't want still exists. So now you have the risk of editors who are squicked out by something in your story and a publisher who'd probably rather not promote it.

Give yourself and your story the best chance possible—sell it to someone who's looking for what you wrote, not someone who needs to be persuaded to make an exception for you.

There's also the issue of the publishing industry being a small world. Editors and other publishing professionals move around from house to house, or they take on freelance clients. It is entirely possible one of the acquisitions editors may move on to another house that you'd like to work with, but they may very well remember you as someone who sees guidelines as a personal challenge, a suggestion, or something to be ignored entirely. None of those options are likely to endear you to a person who is in a position to buy or reject your story.

This isn't so much because you should bow and scrape to industry professionals, or that publishers should never receive pushback about policies. Not at all. It's simply a matter of choosing your battles and deciding whether certain hills are worth dying on and which bridges should be left unburned. Yes, I worked three cliches into one sentence, and no, I'm not sorry about it.

Bottom line, if you find a publisher whose guidelines exclude what you write or have written, or whose guidelines rub you the wrong way, move on. By all means, talk about it with other authors if you think there's a problem with the guidelines—baked-in bigotry, for example—but don't submit out of spite or defiance. This publisher is clearly not the right fit for your work, and your work is clearly not the right fit for them.

Okay. So now we've got that out of the way. We've trimmed down the list of publishers, or maybe you've decided to self-publish.

It's time for everyone's favorite part: editing.

(insert haunted house sounds and someone screaming in the distance)

Yeah, I'm not a fan of editing. It's a necessary part of the process, and I adore my editors who are all worth their weight in gold. It's just not a part of the process I *enjoy*.

(As an aside, it's okay to not enjoy a step in the process. It doesn't make you unprofessional or a bad writer. It just makes you a writer who doesn't enjoy the entire process.)

Anyway. Sometimes writers and editors don't quite match. This doesn't just apply to erotic content, and it doesn't mean either person is bad at their job. I've had some perfectly competent and skilled editors with whom I simply didn't click for any number of reasons.

With erotic content, there can be an added degree of incompatibility. Some editors aren't comfortable with certain content (this applies to a lot of things—violence, political undertones, etc.). Or they may not know much about it (for example, less well-known BDSM practices).

Maybe you prefer somewhat more sensual vocabulary, but your editor prefers more crude language (or vice versa). I had an editor at one point who really, really liked to incorporate "taint" into scenes, whereas I really didn't care for that word.

So, what do you do when you and your editor aren't quite on the same page with sex scenes?

Well, the same thing you do when you're not on the

same page about anything: decide if it's a dealbreaker or if you can work around it.

In my above example about "taint," it was easy to work around. I would just stet the comment, or address whatever she was suggesting without incorporating that word.

By the way, if you're new to working with editors: "Stet" means "let it stand." It's essentially shorthand for, "I'm rejecting your comment/change and leaving the text as it's written." It's a perfectly appropriate response, though your editor may ask for clarification, which is also appropriate— dialogue with your editor is a good thing. And in fact, I've often included an explanation with a Stet comment... and through the course of writing the explanation, talked myself into making the change that was suggested in the first place.

Anyway. Sometimes disagreements really are deal- breakers. If your book contains hardcore BDSM, and your editor isn't comfortable reading—never mind editing— BDSM, they might decline to edit the book. Don't take this as a person being judgmental or looking down on your book (unless they're rude about it, of course). Take it as someone acknowledging they aren't the right person to edit this particular book. There are plenty of people who will!

Sometimes you might have an editor who will edit *most* of what you write, but will decline others. This is okay too. One of my long term editors wasn't comfortable with a particular book because of some difficult political topics. I knew this was a possibility and emailed her ahead of time to ask if she was willing to. She gave it some thought and decided she wasn't. I sent the manuscript to someone else, and she and I continued to work together on other books. Editors have limits and boundaries just like the rest of us.

So what happens if your editor (or beta reader!) says

your manuscript needs more or less sex? Are they right or wrong?

Well, it depends.

Specifically, it depends on *why* they're making that suggestion.

- Would an additional sex scene enhance the story? Or has it just been too many chapters since somebody got naked?
- Is the sex scene they want you to cut too similar to another? Would your story lose anything if you cut that scene?
- Was there a purpose the scene was supposed to serve that it failed to do? Could the scene be edited to serve that purpose, or would it be better to cut it and move on?
- Or does your editor just think that an arbitrary number of sex scenes is too many or too few?

Remember that you can always ask why an editor wants to make a change. You're not being belligerent—this is a collaborative process, and it's perfectly reasonable to request an explanation about why this person wants you to change your work. Not because they need to justify themselves, but because both parties should understand what they're doing.

At the end of the day, sex scenes and erotic content should serve a book the same way any other scene or theme should. Find professionals who want to work with your content, rather than pushing back against those who don't.

As I said, I can go on for an entire book about publishing and editing, but hopefully I've touched on the most salient points.

To recap:

- Do your due diligence and research publishers and/or self-publishing.
- The editorial process is a collaborative one, and both parties should be on the same page.
- Not everyone is comfortable with sex scenes or with all kinds of sex scenes—work with those who are, and respect boundaries and limits.

CHAPTER 10

PLEASE KEEP ALL ARMS, LEGS, AND MISCELLANEOUS APPENDAGES INSIDE THE BUS:
CHOREOGRAPHING YOUR SEX SCENES

Pantsers and other non-planners and non-outliners, hear me out.

I know, I know. A lot of y'all are going to push back on this because you're not a fan of plotting, and because it really seems like plotting and planning will make a sex scene sound mechanical.

But seriously—hear me out. I suspect you will have a much easier time writing (not to mention revising) your scene if you plan it (even vaguely) first. I'd also recommend keeping track of who's had an orgasm and when. It sounds so methodical and unromantic, I know, but if you make all your notes and diagrams at this stage, you won't have readers wondering how one character came three times in two paragraphs without passing out, or being offended on behalf of the poor character who never got off at all.

I also recommend keeping tabs on who's penetrated whom, particularly if there is anal penetration involved. It's up to you to decide if you want your characters to go ass-to-mouth, and I'm not here to debate whether they should or should not. However, much like we'll discuss in the sand-in-a-crack chapter, it's something some of your readers will absolutely notice. It's your decision whether oral-after-anal is going to happen in your scene—just make sure you don't have *accidental* ass-to-mouth simply because you lost track of whose cock or fingers have been where.

If the idea of preplanning or plotting absolutely won't fly with you, I urge you to read anyway, because I have some tips that probably will work for you.

Sex scenes have a lot of moving parts. And I mean that quite literally. It is extraordinarily easy for your characters to sprout additional body parts. Which, okay, that might work in your world, but let's assume that the scene you're writing involves a finite number of established body parts. Ideally, you'll want to keep it that way through the entire scene.

By the same token, even if the climate or fashion mean your characters are dressing in layers, it is generally assumed that they're wearing one pair of jeans, one set of underwear, one bra, etc. When your character takes off their bra for the second time in one scene, your reader is quite possibly and understandably going to look at the scene askance.

This is where planning comes in.

Right up front, I'm going to say this: if you make a mistake with choreography, you're not a failure and you're not alone. I can't tell you how many times I've been editing one of my sex scenes—one I planned to the letter, no less!—and found someone doing something impossible like holding eye contact during doggy style in a story that *didn't* involve an exorcism.

Part I
But when I plan out my scenes,

they sound mechanical.

To put it perfectly bluntly, if a sex scene sounds mechanical, it's not because you planned it out. It's because you wrote it in a way that sounds mechanical.

I'm not saying that to be mean. I've done it myself, and it's a tough thing to break through. It's a difficult mindset, writing something that's meant to be sensual and emotional while focusing on the proverbial nuts and bolts.

Yes, it's great when we can get fully into the moment and write. But the reality is that oftentimes, writing means thinking about the mechanics and movement first.

It's a little like an animatronic dinosaur. They look incredibly real. They're super convincing. But they're built from the inside out. First a blueprint. Then a mechanical skeleton. Then the skin. It's a tedious, technical process, and the end result is something that looks like a living, breathing organism.

Did I just compare writing sex scenes to building animatronic dinosaurs? Yes. Yes, I did. Because that's how I roll.

So let's get to work and build a believable T-Rex.

To start with...

- What do you want to accomplish with this scene?
- Is there a particular emotional outcome you're aiming for?
- Do you want it to go right?
- Do you want it to go wrong?
- Should the tone be light and fun?
- Or heavy on emotion?

From there, it depends on your preferred method. Maybe you plot it out with bullet points. Or maybe you quickly sketch it out with a summary. It can be as sparse or detailed as you need, but especially with more complex scenes, it's a *lot* easier to plan it out first than it is try to keep all the plates spinning while you write. Or to assemble your T-Rex from a pile of parts with no plan and just a vague idea that you want to end up with an animatronic dinosaur.

Remember to apply everything you've learned in the previous chapters to avoid repetition and keeping your scenes interesting.

Part II
I'm not going to plan out my scene, and you can't make me!

Okay, okay. If plotting out a scene really won't work for you, then that's fine. Everyone has their process.

That being said, there are still ways to keep track of the moving parts as you go.

One option is to use a comment bubble to flag certain things. John takes his pants off? Comment bubble. Jordan has an orgasm? Comment bubble.

Or highlight them in different colors.

Basically, find the best visual to keep track of certain things that you don't want repeated. It sounds tedious, I know, but it is ridiculously easy to lose track of limbs, have someone sprout a third hand, or take off their pants twice. Don't worry—we've all done it.

In addition to comment bubbles, you can try a number of different approaches:

- Dolls. Those bendy dolls that artists use can be great for keeping track of who's doing what to whom. I would recommend taking them off the coffee table before Grandma arrives for dinner, though.
- Diagrams. A little more time-consuming than dolls, but it gets the job done.
- Keep score. On a notepad, jot down the very basic play-by-play as you go. When a character moves—even if it's a small move—make a note of it.

At the very least, I encourage you to, upon finishing a sex scene, give it a read-through *solely* to look for mysteriously multiplying limbs or articles of clothing, extra orgasms, or other lapses in choreography.

To recap:

- Planning is your friend.
- Don't lose track of body parts.
- If it seems mechanical, fall back on everything you've learned about writing sex to keep it fresh and interesting.

CHAPTER 11

WHAT ARE YOU LAUGHING AT?

HUMOR IN SEX SCENES

Humor? In a sex scene? Really?

Yes. 1000 times, yes.

Obviously the moment is not always right for levity, but don't overlook how much humor can *elevate* a sex scene.

To explain this, let me take a step back to one of the very basic things every writer has ever had pounded into their head:

SHOW, DON'T TELL.

Of course this isn't a rule, never mind one that can't be broken—there is absolutely a time and a place for telling—but the general idea is a sound one. I won't go into a million pages of explanation about this principle, but stick with me here. Let's take a very quick look at the difference between showing and telling.

Telling: Bob was angry.

Showing: Bob slammed the door and shouted a few curses as he stomped down the walk, ready to beat Phil within an inch of his life.

With that in mind, how do we apply it to humor in sex scenes?

Here's the thing—sex makes people extraordinarily vulnerable. Someone laughing or joking in that scenario can have a very significant impact on the scene itself, whether it continues, and how it continues. Humor between the characters is going to show the reader a great deal about each character's state of mind and/or their relationship dynamic.

Humor in this type of scene can show how intimate and comfortable your characters are with each other. For example, let's say you have a couple who were extremely nervous during their first sex scene. They were each so afraid of disappointing their partner, of not performing well, or screwing up their one chance with this person, and it came through in everything they did. Now, however many chapters later, they're secure in their relationship and completely confident with their partner, and now they're bantering and giggling between the sheets. You have likely spent all those chapters showing their dynamic evolving, and this will underscore how far they've come as a couple.

And this doesn't have to be exclusively romantic intimacy! You can have a pair of friends with benefits who have a chill, easygoing vibe between them, which shows in bed through bantering and making jokes. In whatever context, humor can show the ease of the dynamic between your characters.

The possibilities are endless, honestly.

Here is an example from my book *Bouncing Back*. Samir, the POV character, is trying to move on after an abusive relationship. He's used to walking on eggshells and every encounter—in bed and otherwise—being tense and miserable. In this scene, he's hooking up with Elliott for the first time.

I was enveloped in him. Wrapped up in his arms. Under his broad, strong body. My legs tangled with his. Everywhere we could touch, we did. Every place he could warm just by being there, he did. We rocked together like one of us was already inside the other, cock rubbing cock, skin rubbing skin, and his kiss... Fuck, his *kiss*.

Elliott froze. He lifted his head. His expression wasn't one of panic, but there was definitely some surprise and concern. "Uh, Samir?"

"Hmm?"

"I think... I think there's a cat on my back."

I craned my neck a little, and sure enough, Nima was looking down at me, eyes wide like *hey Dad, what are you doing?* I snapped my fingers, and he got down.

Elliott and I met each other's gazes.

And burst out laughing. He let his head fall against my collarbone, and I clapped a hand over my eyes, and we laughed at the absurdity of the whole thing. Fucking Bengals, man.

I swore I nearly broke down crying, too. Sex and kissing and being turned on were spectacular, but when was the last time I'd *laughed* with someone in bed? I could remember feeling alone, wishing I was alone, crying into my pillow, trying really hard not to cry so I wouldn't wake up the man sleeping next to me and make things worse. But laughing? No.

Fortunately, I kept myself together, and when Elliott lifted his head and found my lips again, it didn't take long for us to go right back from cracking up to making out. This position was perfect, too—with him on top of me like this, both my hands were free to roam his gorgeous body.

- Bouncing Back

The humor—in this case, a pet interrupting them—breaks some tension, and it also drives home to Samir how different this man is from his ex. It shows Samir's state of mind, how easygoing Elliott is, and how relieved Samir is to be putting his awful past behind him. The rest of the sex scene can then proceed without him worrying quite as much as he was before his cat showed up and made them laugh.

There is also the tone of the book to consider. I've read some light, breezy romances peppered with one-liners and snark, but then the sex scenes are what I can only describe as serious. No humor. No banter. None of the playfulness that comes through whenever the characters are dressed.

Sometimes this works. If the sex scene is emotionally charged in ways the rest of the book hasn't been, then the change in dynamic makes sense. For example, if they nearly broke up, or if one partner was missing or in danger, and the sex scene involves emotions that don't really lend themselves to levity. That makes perfect sense. But if everything leading up to and following the sex is light and playful, while the sex reads like something super serious, it *can* feel... out of character.

Don't be afraid to keep that playful spark going when the characters get into bed. In fact, context permitting, I'd encourage you to intensify that spark. Silliness in the bedroom is incredibly underrated, and it truly can take your scene—and the relationship between your characters—to another level.

For example, in this scene, Julien is topping Isaac for the first time, but they have to stay quiet because there are other people in the house:

I trusted Julien and I trusted myself. And if I'd had any doubts left that he'd top me with the same attentiveness and enthusiasm as he bottomed, those had vanished while he'd been driving me wild with his tongue.

"Hey." He slid his palm up my back. "You all right?"

"Yeah." I twisted around to glance at him. "Just...nervous, I guess?" That wasn't a lie. I wasn't afraid of Julien at all, but I *was* nervous.

"I'll go slow." He paused, then added a bratty, "Kind of have to, since we can't make noise."

I snorted. "Shut up and put your dick in me."

He laughed loud enough it probably could have been heard elsewhere in the house, then immediately clapped a hand over his mouth. I had to do the same as we both stifled more laughter.

- Rookie Mistake
Co-written with Anna Zabo

In this instance, the humor shows their easy dynamic, and it also lightens a moment in which one character is nervous.

If you're writing romantic suspense or some other genre that has high stakes and sexual tension, a good laugh during a sex scene can very effectively signal that your characters are safe. Or at least that they feel safe in that moment—if my characters are that relaxed and safe during a sex scene, you can pretty much bet that everything's going to hit the fan in the next chapter. But in the moment, it gives both the reader and the characters a chance to exhale.

So when you've got two people seizing an opportunity for some downtime during a high-stakes action-packed story, humor is a valuable tool that can show the reader just how much it's okay for everyone to release their breath. Ideally enough to let their guard down so the disaster on the next page has more of a kick, but that depends on the story, of course.

Nervous laughter is also a thing. This is something you can absolutely use to your advantage with an inexperienced character, especially a virgin. Self-deprecating comments about their lack of skill. Nervous giggling. Laughing because something is ticklish or a sensation is overwhelming. A joke to lighten the mood that ends up making things awkward.

These all subsequently open up possibilities with regard to the character's partner. Do they make jokes to try to put the person at ease? Do they get defensive and think the person is making fun of them? Do they pick up on the nerves and tap the brakes, soothing and reassuring the person until they're sure they can continue? Do they make the situation better or worse?

Indeed there are millions of scenarios and contexts in which humor in a sex scene can be useful, just as there are millions where it can be out of place and inappropriate. It may or may not work for your story, your characters, or your scene.

To recap:

- Don't overlook humor as a way to enhance a sex scene.

CHAPTER 12

INSERT TAB A INTO... UH-OH
MY CHARACTER & I DON'T HAVE THE SAME PARTS!

Things I've never done before:

- Been shot or even shot at.
- Experienced combat-related PTSD.
- Been bitten by a small shark.
- Shattered an ankle.
- Fought in an arena as a gladiator.
- Done a HALO jump over hostile territory.
- Engaged in a high-speed car chase.
- Had the bends.
- Been tased.
- Snorted cocaine.
- Played ice hockey.

Guess what *else* all of these things have in common?

Yep—I've written all of them at least once. Some many times!

Similarly, I have never owned a penis, a prostate, or a set of testicles. A significant number of my characters have. And they've used them on-page. Successfully!

Every day, we write about things we haven't experienced firsthand, and sex doesn't need to be an exception. What if you've never been with someone who has a vagina? What if you've never been with someone who has a penis? What if you've never had anal, or never topped, or never bottomed, or never experienced prostate stimulation? What if you've never been flogged, or you've never been intimate with someone at all?

That's okay!

You can still write these things... but remember that, like anything else you've never experienced firsthand, you need to do your homework. Be realistic about what you know and what you don't know, and do the legwork to fill in the gaps.

When in doubt... ask. Try Google. If you have a friend who you're comfortable asking—and who is comfortable answering—try picking their brain. Read nonfiction and self-help books and articles about the sex acts, physical configuration, pairings, etc., directed at the people you want to write about. Read about masturbation for someone with different parts. Read novels and stories written by and about people like your characters.

Empathy goes a long way. It's how we're able to write about people who aren't us. But remember it's not just for understanding someone enough to write them believably—it's for understanding someone enough to write them *sensitively*. It's easy to fall into the trap of thinking we understand someone, and therefore have carte blanche to write their stories, when in fact we're making a lot of assumptions. So... be mindful, and remember that you're writing about people.

Beta readers and sensitivity readers are super helpful here, too. Ideally, find betas who are willing to be candid and honest with you about your mistakes, and don't take it personally if they correct something. You're writing outside your experience, so mistakes are bound to occur! Just be open to criticism and course correct as you go. Also, it's very common and appropriate for sensitivity readers to charge for their service; make sure you're in agreement ahead of time about how much they charge, when the payment is due, and how it will be remitted.

To actually explain the mechanics of how sex works with various physical configurations and pairings would make this book incredibly long, and I think I would be stepping well out of my lane at that point. What I will do is list some book recommendations after the last chapter to help you in that regard.

But the major takeaway from this brief chapter is...

- Be honest with yourself about the limitations of your own experience.
- Research what you don't know.
- When you think you understand it, research some more.
- Be respectful to the people you're writing about.
- Sensitivity readers are your friend.

CHAPTER 13

I'M NOT SO SURE ABOUT THIS
WRITING SEX SCENES OUTSIDE YOUR COMFORT ZONE

If you write enough erotic content, there may very well come a scene where the hottest, most believable, and most in-character thing is outside your comfort zone. It could be something you don't enjoy in real life or find off-putting to watch. It could be something that full-on makes your skin crawl due to a phobia, a bad experience, or simply your own tastes.

To be clear, I'm not talking about anything that's abusive, harmful, or illegal here—I just mean things that may fit for your scene, but aren't...well, aren't your scene. Maybe your character is kinkier than you. Maybe they enjoy topping while you're exclusively a bottom. You don't have to like everything your characters do.

So let's talk about some reasons why you might not enjoy writing a particular act:

- **Personal experience**. Anything from simply realizing it does nothing for you to a truly bad experience or a trauma.
- **Lack of experience**. You've never tried it, so

you have no frame of reference to determine how it would feel or what it would be like.

- **Inability to experience**. You don't have a penis but want to write about receiving a blowjob. You've never performed cunnilingus but want to write a character who's doing so.
- **Discomfort/squick**. This is a perfectly valid thing, and not something to be ashamed of. We all have things we like and don't like.

In a later chapter, I'll get into writing about things you either have not experienced or cannot experience firsthand. This chapter will mostly focus on squicks, discomfort, and trauma.

First, know your limits. If something is genuinely traumatic or triggering for you, consider whether the story you're telling is worth what you'll put yourself through. Maybe it'll be cathartic and therapeutic for you. That's fine. But if writing it will cause you more distress than it's worth, you *do not have to write it*. I say this as someone who's had to put a few books on hold because a scene or a theme hit too close to the bone. There's no shame in it. We all suffer for our art to some degree, but you don't have to *literally* suffer for it.

Beyond traumas and triggers, there may still be things you are either uncomfortable writing or flat out refuse to write. And I want to say right now that just like with traumas and triggers, it is one hundred percent okay to have hard limits. I have such a deep secondhand embarrassment squick that I cannot stomach watching the bad audition scenes on shows like American Idol. I get horribly uncomfortable just watching a character on a sitcom being embarrassed or awkward. As a result, I *will not* write humiliation scenes even though I write a fair amount of BDSM.

Other limits aren't quite as firm. Certain types of breath play (choking or otherwise cutting off air) are difficult for me to write because I have a pretty significant phobia about things around my neck, but I can write them. I just have to be in the right frame of mind to do so.

This isn't all that unusual. I know one writer who struggles to write deep-throating because just writing it triggers her gag reflex. Another finds anal sex to be horrendously uncomfortable, but can write it like someone who thinks bottoming is the most amazing thing ever. Still another is claustrophobic and cannot cope with being restrained or immobile, but can write extreme bondage scenes like nobody else.

If you're struggling to write something, but you know it belongs in your story, ease into it. For example, let's say you want to write a cunnilingus scene, but it's not your thing, and you're not entirely comfortable writing it. Start with a scene from the POV of the person receiving. This doesn't have to be a scene that winds up in your book, by the way—just one you write to get a feel for it. Describe how your POV character feels instead of a play-by-play of what their partner is doing. Alternatively, write a scene where your POV character is watching another character perform the act. In neither of these scenes do you need to go into graphic detail about the actual cunnilingus.

One thing that is outside my comfort zone is rimming. I know there are plenty of people who absolutely love giving it, receiving it, watching it, writing about it, and reading about it, but I'm not one of them. It's not a question of judging those who do it—much like humiliation or breath play, it's simply something that isn't for me, and I struggled to write it. So for a long time, I just... didn't.

I write a lot of sex between men, though, and rimming is a common enough practice that I felt its total absence in my work was becoming conspicuous. I needed to be true to my characters, and I needed my characters and their experiences to be authentic. For some men who have sex with men, rimming is a thing they enjoy, either giving, receiving, or both. So, I started including it, and I worked very hard to keep my own personal feelings about it from coming through, because I wanted my scenes to be authentic and respectful.

As I was beginning to overcome my hang-ups, I found it much easier to write from the POV of a person receiving it than giving it, so that's what I did:

His hands slid over my buttocks, and I bit my lip, not sure what to expect. Fingers first, I guessed. Something to relax me, get me used to contact before he asked me to take his cock.

What I didn't expect was his tongue.

I jumped, my entire body stiffening. It wasn't unpleasant—far from it—just...different. As foreign as any sensation could be, but so, so arousing.

The tip of his tongue circled slowly, first one way, then the other. My entire body tingled with the barrage of sensations radiating from that one incredible point of contact. It went from strange and alien to downright addictive, and I silently begged him not to stop. Never to stop.

My head spun. The edges of my vision darkened. Then I sucked in a breath and realized I hadn't done so in far too long. It wasn't that I couldn't breathe, I'd just forgotten to.

Scott stopped. "You all right?" The playful lilt told me he knew full well I was fine.

- For the Living

When I became more confident in my ability to write rimming, I stepped up to writing it from the POV of the person giving:

While I get the condom and lube, he turns onto his hands and knees. Of course, he's impossibly sexy like that, offering up his ass to me. I don't even have the wrapper open yet, and I already can't wait.

I move behind him and put the condom and bottle aside. Then I take his ass cheeks in my hands and push them apart, and run my tongue along the crack.

"Holy—" He bucks against me, and when I do it again, he makes a choked sound.

"Like that?" I ask.

"Yeah. Ungh. God."

I grin, then go in for more. I tease his hole with my tongue, alternately circling and probing, and he presses back against me as if looking for more. It's been ages since I've done this, never mind with someone as enthusiastic and vocal, and I can't get enough. Not when he's moaning and squirming like that every time I touch him. Fuck him till he cries? Sign me the hell up.

I keep one hand on his ass and slip the other between his legs. With the lightest possible touch of my fingertips, I tease his balls.

"Max..." He whimpers. "Max, c'mon. Fuck...fuck me."

Oh, I want to, and I will, but his breathless pleading is too hot for words. I keep tonguing him, keep teasing his balls, and he keeps right on whispering my name between moans and shivers.

- *At the Corner of Rock Bottom & Nowhere*

Even here, there's actually very little specific detail about what Max is doing with his tongue, but there's enough for the reader to be fully engaged and understand why both men are responding the way they do.

The idea is to be cognizant of your squicks, own them, and understand they *can* come through in your writing. If you absolutely can't keep the squick from showing through, find a way around writing it. You're better off leaving something out than writing it in such a way that makes the reader —someone who might enjoy that particular thing—feel gross, or like you're making fun of or judging them and something they enjoy.

It's also worth noting that you don't need to go into extremely graphic detail on *anything* your characters are doing, regardless of whether they're doing something you enjoy. You certainly can go into extreme detail if it fits the scene, the tone, etc., but don't feel like you need a blow-by-blow (so to speak) description of every single thing that's happening. The mechanics aren't nearly as interesting as the effects—your reader will squirm when your character squirms, and they'll lose interest if the focus is on body parts and nothing else.

Case in point, refer back to the examples above in which I wrote rimming despite it being outside my comfort zone. There isn't a tremendous amount of description of the actual act—it's all about the sensations and responses.

A final note—if a particular act bothers you enough that your feelings make it into the writing, err on the side of leaving it out. If anal sex grosses you out so much that the scene *reads* like it's written by someone grossed out by anal sex... don't write anal sex. Respect yourself, your characters, your readers, and real-life people who enjoy things you don't.

To recap:

- Write what your character likes and is experiencing.
- You're not endorsing it or announcing that you practice it.
- If you absolutely can't write it without your discomfort coming through, you're probably better off not writing it.
- Know and respect your own limits.

Now, let's move on to your characters' technique...

PART 2

PHYSICS, PHYSIOLOGY, PHALLUSES, & FANTASY

In sex scenes—and indeed romantic and erotic fiction—fantasy and reality often diverge, and it can be difficult to strike a balance between the two: enough fantasy to make it fun with enough reality to keep the reader grounded in the scene.

How do we as writers strike that balance?

Well, let's talk about some things that can challenge a reader's suspension of disbelief, if not throw them out of the scene entirely.

CHAPTER 1

THAT'S GONNA STAIN

WHEN THINGS GET MESSY

Yep, we're gonna go there.

Let's face it—sex is messy. As much as we try to gloss over it in order to keep that airbrushed perfection we see in the movies, the reality is that it involves bodies and bodily fluids.

So how much should we include in our scenes?

Well, as with anything, it depends on the story, the scene, etc. In general, though, there is a balance to be struck between glossing over and overlooking. Fortunately, that's easier than it sounds.

In the real world, sex usually involves some clean-up afterward. For certain practices, there's often prep beforehand. Your reader knows that. So how much do you show on page?

In my opinion, it doesn't hurt to keep it realistic enough that it feels real to the reader, but it's okay to gloss over the less attractive bits. You don't need to include a play-by-play of pre-anal enemas, just like you don't need to show someone peeing after sex so they don't get a UTI. Bodies make less than flattering sounds sometimes, especially if air or liquid gets trapped somewhere. Leaving those sounds out of your sex scenes won't make them any less believable, but including them might kill the effect you're trying to have.

If you *want* to include the messy parts, and that works for your scene and your story, then by all means, include them. You are the writer, and it is ultimately up to you what belongs in a scene or what doesn't.

But just know that you don't *have* to include them in the name of realism. Your reader is smart—they know your characters do a lot of things that you don't show on-screen. You don't have to spell out your character using the bathroom, tying their shoes, or folding their laundry, and your readers can put two and two together with sex scenes too.

At the same time, though it may seem a bit paradoxical, if you *don't* touch on certain aspects, your reader might spend the rest of the scene wondering what happened.

- *Is he ever going to take off that condom?*
- *They went bareback, so that cum's going to make a reappearance eventually.*
- *You're just gonna fall asleep without even —really?*

So is it possible to address these things without detailing the squelchy parts? Absolutely!

One method? The well-placed scene break. End the sex scene before the characters shift gears from getting it on to cleaning it up. Then pick up the next scene with them cuddling in bed or relaxing on the couch or what have you, maybe mentioning that someone's hair is still damp from the shower they'd shared. You can pick up the scene with something like "After they'd cleaned up..." The point is to show a jump past the time between the sex and the cleaned-up state, giving it a little hat tip to acknowledge it happened without the play by play.

You can also address things with an offhand comment. For example, a character can gesture at a condom and say, "I'm going to go take care of this. Be right back." Or if two characters are going to have anal sex, no one needs to list every step they took to prep ahead of time. The bottom can flirtatiously tell the top, "I'm ready for you and everything."

This was actually something I got hung up on early in my career. For whatever reason, I felt like I needed to show my characters *all* the way through the sex scene and the post-coital cuddling. But then I realized, not how gross that transition is, but how utterly *boring* it can be. Replacing it with a scene break and a brief acknowledgment that cleanup had occurred did wonders for my pacing.

That's really all you really need. Now your characters can move on and the reader isn't left wondering if anything is sticky. Essentially, when you encounter things you don't want to explicitly show on-page, but that your reader will likely notice if they're obviously missing, make space for them to happen off-camera. Readers who don't care won't notice either way. Those who do will be assured that your characters are cognizant of hygiene.

Another thing to keep in mind is that even though fiction is fantasy, it doesn't take much for elements to add up to something that pulls the reader out of the story and makes them think, "Oh Lord. No. That's not sexy." Sometimes that's what you want, and that's fine, but in contexts where you don't want to squick out your reader, this is important to consider.

If your characters have just gorged themselves on a seven-course meal, and now they want to have rough, acrobatic sex, there's a definite possibility your reader might worry about someone getting sick. Or if the characters just ate something seriously spicy—well, that can have a number of effects that might make your reader think "Oh, that's hot" in a way you didn't intend. There are a number of ways diet can come into play with anal sex in particular. If these aren't things you want your reader to think about while reading your sex scene, make sure you're considering every angle. It's your job as the writer to think about these things so your reader doesn't have to.

Food isn't the only thing to take into consideration pre-sex. If your characters have been hiking all day long and have finally made camp in the desert after a week of traveling in the same clothes, I can get onboard with them having sex... but unless there's some magically pristine spring nearby that your characters have mentioned bathing in, oral sex *might* not be the best choice.

The jury seems to be out on whether things like enemas are necessary prior to anal. Every time I read an article in favor of them or talk to a gay man who swears by them, I read another article or talk to another guy who thinks they're unnecessary or even harmful. I'm not here to debate the subject, though. In terms of writing romance, it's not a question of whether something needs to happen—it's a question of whether it needs to happen *on-page*. We don't have to spell out a character preventing a UTI by getting up to pee after sex, and we don't have to detail pre-anal practices either.

That's not to say enemas or any other practices are gross or shameful. They just might not fit well with your sex scene. If they do, have at it. If you'd prefer to keep it subtle or gloss over it, that can be as simple as giving the character an obvious opportunity, such as mentioning the character has freshly showered.

So what about the aftermath?

Look, sex is messy. If lube and semen go in, they're going to come out. Condoms have to be disposed of. Tissues, towels, or washcloths might be needed.

How much do you describe? As with everything, that's up to you. My usual MO with the aftermath of any sex scene is to mention in passing that the characters cleaned themselves up, and leave it at that. You can have one character lovingly or subserviently—depending on the relationship—clean the other off. You can go into detail about fluids and such. It really depends on what you're going for in your scene.

Sometimes, possibly in the name of realism, a writer will conclude a sex scene by going into graphic detail about everything that's being wiped up/off/out. And while it's certainly realistic, you'll want to consider if it'll be jarring to the reader to go from deliciously hot sex to an intricate description of cum globs on a wad of toilet paper.

Point being, there is a balance to be struck between glossing over the gross parts and overlooking them to the point they actually stick out to your *reader*.

To recap:

- Consider your sex scenes within the context of the scenes before and after them.
- Make space for characters to take care of anything that's necessary but not something you want to explicitly include in your scene (prep, cleanup, etc.).
- It's our job as writers to consider all the unpleasant possibilities so our reader doesn't have to.

CHAPTER 2

FAILURE TO LAUNCH
WHEN THINGS DON'T GO AS PLANNED

When I first began writing sex, I had this idea that every sex scene had to be perfect. As in, the characters had to do everything right, everybody had to get off, and it was all bliss and sunshine afterward.

Turns out that isn't the case. Sex is messy and sometimes clumsy, and sometimes it doesn't go as flawlessly as we'd all like it to. Sometimes it's over before it starts, or something unexpected interrupts the moment. Fiction can absolutely reflect this chaos; in fact, some of the most poignant and powerful sex scenes out there are as messy and imperfect as real life. They can show a character or relationship's resiliency, or they can shine a bright light on problems brewing beneath the surface.

If you take away one thing and one thing only from this book, let it be this:

Don't underestimate the power and versatility of a failed sex scene.

For starters, they can increase tension. While sex scenes themselves generally relieve sexual tension, an interrupted sex scene has the exact opposite effect. More than one interrupted sex scene increases that tension exponentially. My co-writer Cari Z and I once had an editor tell us that if we cockblocked our characters *one more time*, she was going to scream—not because it was bad, but because we had quite intentionally cranked up the sexual tension until both characters were about to burst into flames. A great deal of this was accomplished purely by interrupting them every time they tried to do anything.

I broke the kiss and went for his neck because it had been too long since I'd done that to anyone, and holy fuck, it was as amazing as I remembered. The warmth of his skin against my lips. The vibration of his voice when he moaned. The way he tilted his head so I could kiss anywhere and everywhere.

And right fucking then, my phone came to life in my pocket.

We both froze.

I swore under my breath and dug the damn thing out. The caller ID said it was the captain. My dick said he could wait.

I hit Ignore and tossed the phone onto another cushion.

"Not important?" he asked.

"Not even a little." I kissed his neck again, and he didn't ask questions.

But then another muffled sound interrupted us —the "Bad Boys" theme from *COPS*.

"Motherfucker," Darren grumbled. He reached for his own pocket.

"The *COPS* theme? Really?"

"Eh." He shrugged as he took it out. "Shit. It's the captain."

I groaned, scrubbing a hand over my face. Of course it was.

-Risky Behavior
co-written with Cari Z

Don't overlook the power of the cockblock. Nothing cranks up sexual tension like the characters being into it and ready to go, and then interrupted.

It doesn't always have to be completely interrupted, though. Sometimes things happen, and characters need to adapt to new circumstances. In this example, the two characters have just left a big showdown with the villain, and they desperately want to connect with each other physically. But the evening they've already had is still affecting both of them, especially Jesse, and it becomes clear that the night isn't going to go as planned.

"You sure you want me on top tonight?"

"Yes." He arched under my hand and murmured over his shoulder, "God, I want you, Hayden."

I shivered from the raw desire in his unsteady voice, and somehow managed to keep my own voice even. "I know you do. But I don't want to hurt you."

"You won't. Just... just go slow."

"You know I will." I silently debated calling this off, but he wanted it. Really wanted it. And, I mean, I'd topped a few guys who'd never bottomed before, and nothing made a man clench up tighter than nerves. With a few gallons of lube and some serious patience, they could usually relax enough to take me.

So I cautiously pressed on. I eased a fingertip into him, and his moan definitely wasn't one of protest or pain. In fact he leaned back, searching for more, and I let him impale himself on my finger. After a while, I carefully added a second finger. Then some more lube.

"Like that?" I asked.

He nodded soundlessly. He kept rocking back and forth, setting a slow, fluid rhythm. A shiver ran up his spine, and he murmured, "I want more."

I chewed my lip. Yeah, he probably wanted more. Question was, could he *take* more? As it was, he was so tight it was almost painful for me, and while I'm not exactly hung like a porn star, my dick *is* longer and thicker than two fingers. If he was this tight around my fingers—okay, he might be able to take me, but I didn't see how he'd enjoy it. Even if he could relax enough for me to get into him, it wouldn't be comfortable, and while I was absolutely ready and willing to do anything he needed for him, there were lines I wouldn't cross.

So I slid my fingers free.

"Jesse." I shook my head. "This isn't working. If I try to top you, I'm just going to hurt you."

"It's fine," he insisted over his shoulder. "Just go slow."

"No. You're too tense." I realized a second too late that in his raw, battered mental state, that probably sounded like *we can't do this and it's your fault.* "Turn around." When he did, I touched his chin and lifted it so he was looking in my eyes. "You've had a hell of a night, and anyone would be wound up after that. I just don't want to hurt you."

He pursed his lips, disappointment and shame radiating off him. "I want you tonight."

"And you've got me." I ran the pad of my thumb over his unbruised cheekbone. "I don't care if we can't fuck. We'll get there again. I'm not here for your ass, Jesse—I'm here for you. I'm not going anywhere."

- The Husband Gambit

This is an example of a scene in which the characters can still have sex, just not the way they wanted to. Jesse is too tense thanks to his stressful night, and Hayden recognizes that they're better off finding other ways to satisfy each other instead of doing something that will hurt his partner. Their failure is frustrating in the moment, but it leads them to a more poignant scene that shows not only how much they desire each other, but how much they *care* for each other.

Along the same lines, I've also written characters who had to stop or change direction because of physical pain due to injuries, including several who experience chronic pain, which I'll touch on in another chapter. This creates a scenario in which their partner can reveal themselves to be deeply caring and compassionate, or they can respond badly and create negative tension going forward. In such an intimate, vulnerable situation, there is serious potential for a character's reaction to be perfect, disastrous, or anything in between.

On a similar note, it's possible to get characters into bed, only to have them realize they don't really want to be there. Maybe they're not ready to have sex, either with this person or at all. Maybe they're too distracted or upset about something else.

Or maybe they're in bed with someone they don't want to have sex with. In this scene, Shahid and his husband, Gabe, are trying to have a baby with their friend Kendra. While Gabe is bisexual and hasn't had any difficulty sleeping with Kendra, Shahid is gay. But he does want a chance at fathering their child, and he's never been with a woman. Plus, he's feeling a bit weird about sharing his husband, and he's starting to feel like a third wheel in his own bed.

So, he and Kendra give it a chance together. Or, well, they try to.

Nerves fluttered in my stomach, but I ignored them as she rolled on her back and I moved on top of her. She parted her legs for me, and with her help, I guided myself in. Slowly, I pushed into her.

Kendra closed her eyes. I exhaled. She was tight, but she took me easily, and my head spun as I began to move inside her, taking long, slow strokes.

This felt great, but was I being honest with myself? With her? She was pretty, and she knew how to touch a man, but there wasn't that mind-bending chemistry between us. Curiosity had brought us this far. Could it—

Quit overthinking it.

Was I overthinking it? Panic shot through me. What if I couldn't finish?

Think of Gabe.

My husband's gorgeous naked body and low moans of arousal flashed through my mind, and my spine tingled.

Oh yes. Gabe.

Except now I was lying to her.

And did I need to distract myself?

After all, this didn't feel *bad.* It wasn't... She wasn't...

It was...

Focus, Shahid. Just—

"Shahid?"

I opened my eyes and met hers.

She touched my cheek. "You're really not into this, are you?"

"I..."

"It's okay." She smiled. "Don't force it."

My face burned as I pulled out and eased myself down beside her. "I am so sorry. I—"

"Don't apologize. You can't make yourself want this if you don't." She paused and glanced down. Then she pulled the covers up to her collarbones. "Should I, um, get dressed? Or—"

"You don't have to."

"Really? But..." She gestured at our naked bodies.

"It's okay. I mean, I'm not disgusted by women." Fresh heat rushed into my cheeks. "Well, I guess we've answered one question—I am *definitely* gay."

She giggled. "You don't say."

I met her gaze. "I'm sorry. I probably sound awful. It's not you, I promise. I—"

"Shahid." She gently clasped my hand between hers. "I get it. I promise. It's nothing personal. You're gay. I'm a woman." Smiling, she added, "I'm not into women either, so I really do understand."

At that, I relaxed a little.

- The Best Laid Plans

So in this case, the sex fails, but the scene ends up strengthening the bond between Kendra and Shahid. She could have laughed at him, or he could've been too embarrassed to look at her, or things could have otherwise gotten incredibly awkward, but they didn't. This was deliberate on my part because of the jealousy and imbalance in their three-way relationship. Their failure to finish—and the way they handled it—led to less tension between them, but at the same time, it ultimately worsens the imbalance between Shahid, Kendra, and Gabe, which increases the overall tension and gives them more conflict to work out by the end of the book.

Could that have been accomplished without the failed sex scene? Maybe. Maybe not. But this was the approach that made the most sense with these characters and their dynamic. It made them the most vulnerable, which was what I wanted.

As the writer, it's your job to decide which scenes and events are most appropriate and effective for the result you're working toward. Sometimes, that's a sex scene. Sometimes, it's a sex scene that goes awry.

When considering how a failed sex scene can add to a

story, it can absolutely go beyond the characters and their relationships! Want to really get your reader's heart pounding in an action story? Interrupt a much-needed sex scene in a dramatic and unexpected way. In this case, a scene between two vampires and a werewolf doesn't quite play out the way it's supposed to:

I loved the way Levi moved when I was inside him, the way he thrust back against me and the sounds he made, the way he pleaded for more, even when I was fucking him so hard it hurt.

"God, hurry up," Levi moaned, arching and squirming beneath me. "Fuck me."

"I'm getting there," I teased as I stroked on some lube.

He just whimpered again. Ian and I exchanged devilish grins, and I silently promised to fuck him too before this day was over. The trembling said the message was received loud and clear.

Levi lay back on the bed and parted his legs. I guided myself and—

Froze.

Something had grazed my senses. Something that didn't belong.

"Darius?" Levi touched my shoulder. "What's wrong?"

I put up a hand and held my breath, listening to the air around us.

Then Levi started to sit up a little, eyes darting back and forth. Ian slowly turned his head toward the window above the bed.

Their heartbeats both accelerated, and that was

when I figured out what was out of place. Theirs weren't the only heartbeats I heard. There were too many. Our hearts were pounding, but they were nearly in sync with each other. The faint rhythm in the background didn't come from any of us, and it was getting louder. Stronger. *Closer.*

Levi peered around. Then his nose twitched, and I could almost feel his hackles rising.

I took in a breath through my nose. The sharp, pungent sourness on the air immediately burned the insides of my nostrils. I turned to Levi. "Is that..."

"Smoke." He got out of bed.

"Smoke?" Ian's forehead creased. "I don't smell anything."

"You will." Levi picked up Ian's jeans and handed them to him. "Get dressed."

Ian didn't seem convinced, but he didn't say anything as he pulled on his pants. Levi and I did the same, and found our shirts and boots.

"Where exactly are we going?" Ian asked.

"We can't leave," Levi said. "The sun's up."

My heart pounded. Claustrophobia usually only applied to physically tight spaces, but being cornered was being cornered and, holy fuck, we were cornered. The house was surrounded. Any exit not covered by a wolf was covered by the sun.

For Levi's and Ian's sakes, I took a deep breath to bring my heart rate down. "We might not be able to go anywhere, but if anyone decides to come in here..." I pulled on my shirt.

"And what if they do?" Ian asked. "What the hell do we do?"

> Levi shook his head. "I have no—"
> The window above the bed exploded.
>
> ---
>
> *- The United & The Divided*

Because nothing says "maybe later" like a Molotov cocktail landing in your bed.

So don't underestimate how much an interrupted sex scene can do for your story. There are no rules that say a sex scene has to continue to completion. And don't forget how hot it'll be later when they get a chance to pick up where they left off!

While we're driving the reader up a wall, now is a good time to point out that arousing said reader doesn't *need* to be part of the sex scene's goal. It's fun to write a hot scene that gets interrupted, but it's also possible to write very visceral and emotional sex scenes that are more heartbreaking or frustrating than arousing.

> His fingers were wonderfully talented—nimble, gentle, never too rough or too light, and God, but the man knew his way around a woman.
>
> But her orgasm stayed just out of reach, and slowly, the truth settled in: it wasn't going to happen tonight. Her mind was just too far away and in too many other places to let her body surrender completely.
>
> So she gasped, she shuddered, and she dug her nails into his arm, and she didn't give him a single reason to think it wasn't genuine. She lifted her hips off the bed, pressing against his hand, and she

moaned like she meant it. She *did* mean it—he turned her on, and he knew how to please her like no other man ever had—but this was all she had tonight, and she prayed to God he believed her.

As she relaxed, James kissed her softly and withdrew his fingers. Fresh guilt gnawed at her. She'd never been one to fake orgasms, but lately, it was either that or stop and talk about why she couldn't come. And she'd rather fake it than spoil one of these increasingly rare moments of intimacy.

- Kneel, Mr. President

Before this point, the reader has been introduced to the problems brewing between husband and wife, but now they've *felt* those problems. What better way to illustrate the distance between two people than by putting them as close as possible in the most intimate of scenarios and *not* letting them connect?

While we're on the subject of failures to launch, what about erectile dysfunction? Can you write sex scenes involving characters with ED? Absolutely! A hard penis is not the end-all, be-all of sex, and there are plenty of ways people can still enjoy themselves without an erection.

You can also use this to cultivate trust and love between your characters. ED can be incredibly embarrassing and distressing, whether it's a one-time thing or a chronic problem. This can be an opportunity for the character with ED to make themselves vulnerable to their partner. It can also be an opportunity for the partner to show how much they care for and desire the other person.

One of my characters in *Aftermath* has ED thanks to a

serious injury. He discovers this the first time he and the love interest try to have sex, which causes him all manner of embarrassment and frustration. The story then proceeds through them figuring out their intimate life around his ED and severe chronic pain, as well as him exploring treatments and the potential for recovery. While a penis pump—the medical kind available by prescription, not the novelty variety—seems clinical and perhaps unsexy, it's all in how it's used.

The point here is that two loving partners who want to be intimate with each other can adapt to setbacks and still have satisfying sex, and this can still result in sex scenes that are sexy and hot. It's all in how the writer chooses to have their characters respond to whatever complications are thrown their way.

Like I said at the beginning of this chapter:

Don't underestimate the power and versatility of a failed sex scene.

To recap:

- Sex scenes can go awry just like any other scene.
- Not every sex scene needs to be arousing or titillating, and can in fact be extremely effective as the opposite.
- Physical and emotional complications can turn sex scenes into opportunities for characters to demonstrate how much they truly love and care for one another.

CHAPTER 3

PUCKER UP, BUTTERCUP
ALL ABOUT KISSING

Let's.

Talk.

Kissing.

Kissing is sexy. It's hot.

For many people, this is the first physical step toward sex. It's intimate, and it can both turn someone on and convey to the other person how turned on they are. There's a lot to be said for kissing as the gateway to the bedroom, especially in romantic and erotic fiction.

Before we get into that, though, it's also important to note that, for various reasons, some people don't like kissing on the mouth, especially with a person they've just met, a casual hookup, or someone they've hired. For some, it's incredibly intimate. For others, it's as crucial to sex—if not more so—as lube and orgasms. Kissing after oral is an incredible turn-on for some, and it's utterly revolting to others.

There's no right or wrong here—just knowing your characters and being consistent.

Going forward, we're discussing characters who do enjoy kissing on the mouth.

How much should you describe a kiss? Of course that depends. Especially after your characters are already physically established, there's no need to describe every kiss in great detail. You'll kill your pacing, especially in a novel. There is absolutely a time and a place for "he stole a kiss on his way out the door" or "she stopped him in his tracks with a long kiss."

What I would suggest is not passing up the chance to pause and zoom in on the important kisses.

Which kisses are the important ones?

- The first kiss.
- The reunion kiss.
- The "stop talking before I lose it" kiss.
- The "this might be the last time I see you" kiss.
- The "I wish it didn't have to be this way" kiss.
- etc.

When a kiss is significant somehow—when it's intense, when it's powerful, when it's meaningful—don't let it be anticlimactic. This is also a reason to not turn every kiss into An Event—it'll dilute the importance of those that hold more significance.

As far as how much description those important kisses should get, everything that applies to sex scenes applies here, too. Don't just focus on the physical contact. Emotions, emotions, emotions! Sensory details! Make your character's knees shake. Make their heart stop. Make your reader hold their breath in the moments leading up to that first contact.

Movies are a great resource for learning how to write

the tension leading up to a kiss, as well as the sexiness of the kiss itself. Look up clips of the most memorable kisses from film and television. Watch them with and without the sound. Focus on body language, how close they are, how long they linger as they move in (assuming they don't just go for broke). When the kiss happens, watch their hands and bodies, not just their mouths. Watch for furrows in the brow, the way they squeeze their eyes shut. Yeah, it's acting, not a "real" kiss, but remember that what they're doing is a deliberate series of motions to convey emotion, tension, etc., to you, the viewer. Observe what works, and translate that onto the page.

Let's focus on the first kiss for a moment. There are any number of things that can go through a person's head in the moments leading up to a first kiss, during the kiss itself, and immediately after. It can be heady, silly, powerful, emotional, terrifying—it depends on the dynamic you've created and how the scene plays out.

To illustrate, these are the first kisses from three separate books.

Between an inexperienced submissive and the intimidating but attractive Dominant who's piqued his curiosity...

I swallowed. Swept my tongue across my lips. And finally, by some miracle, I whispered a shaky, *"Please."*

I thought my next heartbeat would be a shower of sparks from his lips claiming mine, but he didn't move in. Not yet. He let us hang there a few seconds longer, toes over the edge of the precipice, balance shifting but not quite past the point of no return, my heart pounding and my breath lodged in my throat and more anticipation crackling along my senses than I'd ever known before and—

Lips. Sparks. Oh God.

His hands tightened around my wrists in the same moment his lips softened against mine, and he used his body to keep me upright against the wall as his tongue gently slipped into my mouth. I wanted to wrap my arms around him, but being pinned like this while he kissed me—that was beyond sexy. Even as my fingertips itched with the frustrating absence of touch, my whole body melted in the intense heat of Austin's perfect, languid kiss.

When his forehead touched mine, we were both out of breath, panting hard against each other's lips.

"Do..." I struggled to pull my thoughts together. "Do *everything* to me."

- The Right to Remain

Between a powerful Sicilian gangster and an Irish rum runner who've tried really, really hard to hate each other for half the book but are finally realizing the truth...

Carmine moistened his lips.

Danny looked, and when he met Carmine's gaze again, that glint of something burned even hotter than before.

He couldn't be imagining it. He'd played these wordless games with too many men before to not understand everything Danny was saying without speaking. It was only disbelief that kept him from moving. This couldn't be real. Could it? Danny had hated him at the start. Warmed to him steadily over time. Was it possible he *wanted* Carmine now? That what had begun as warmth had become genuine heat?

Experimentally, Carmine inched forward. Danny tensed, but he didn't give any ground. He stayed put, eyes still locked on Carmine's.

Carmine lifted his chin, and Danny lowered his just slightly, bringing their mouths to the same height, so close someone only needed to lean in or inhale deeply and they'd be touching. And God in heaven, Carmine wanted to feel and taste those lips, but he hesitated, lingering there with his mouth almost grazing Danny's just to feel the electric anticipation.

Then their lips touched, and somehow every light bulb in the room didn't explode in a shower of sparks. Somehow Carmine didn't.

- The Venetian and the Rum Runner

And between a man who has been deeply-closeted and self-loathing for a long time, but is trying to come to terms with his sexuality, and the escort he hasn't been able to bring himself to kiss on the mouth yet...

I met his gaze again. "Up until recently, I've hated myself for wanting men. And for sleeping with men. It probably sounds stupid, but kissing just always seemed too..."

"Too intimate?"

Cheeks warm, I nodded. "I know, it's ridiculous, but—"

"No, I get it. Kissing can be as intimate as sex. Or even more so."

I nodded slowly.

"Have you ever kissed a man before?" he asked.

"Yeah. Long time ago." Even now, the memory of that night with Matt made my stomach twist with shame. Not for what we'd done in bed, though. Not anymore. No, I didn't think I'd ever forgive myself for the way I treated him afterward. I cleared my throat and looked at Hunter. "A really, really long time ago."

"Do you want to now? With me?"

I couldn't resist, and I let my gaze flick to his gorgeous, full lips. Barely whispering, I said, "Yeah. I do."

Our eyes met again. For long heartbeats, we held each other's gazes. I wanted to draw him in or move closer, but nerves had ramped up, and all I could do was silently beg him to cross the distance I couldn't.

Then... he did.

He leaned closer, tilting his head, and my pulse surged. I had a moment of panic—half a second of *wait, no, I can't*—before soft lips met mine.

And the whole world stilled except for my pounding heart.

After long seconds, Hunter gently dragged his lower lip across mine, encouraging mine into motion, and I sighed as I slid my hand up into his hair and let this perfect, tender kiss happen.

This wasn't the first time I'd kissed a man, but it was the first time I'd kissed a man sober. The first time I'd kissed a man *honest.*

He's a man. I want this. I want him.

I'm gay. I really am gay, and...

And this is amazing.

I pulled him in closer. He gave a quiet moan, wrapping his arms around me, and I was not prepared for the barrage of emotions that came crashing in. Shame and guilt were there, of course, because it was a damned habit, but there was so much more. Relief. Need. A feeling like I'd been holding on to something for dear life until my muscles burned with fatigue, and then I'd let go, and the fall was so much less terrifying than I'd convinced myself it would be. It was so *liberating.*

Why didn't I let go sooner?

Escort or not, a kiss wasn't supposed to leave me shaking like this. Like I was ready to fall apart without even really knowing why. Like I'd just tasted something delicious after years of self-imposed starvation and was suddenly hit with the reality of everything I'd robbed myself of and more earthshaking regret than I'd anticipated.

Hunter drew back a little and touched my cheek. "Hey. You okay?"

"Yeah." Why did that feel like a lie?

- Hunter, Gentlemen of the Emerald City, book 6

All three of these are the same in that they are a first kiss, but the scenes are wildly different. The first kiss—and indeed, any kiss—should reflect and enhance the dynamic between the characters that you've been building in the pages leading up to it. The exception to this is when you're using that kiss to shift the dynamic. When the kiss is a turning point—the catalyst for new emotions and a new way of interacting—then obviously there will be some differences. But if your characters hate each other, and then they kiss and are suddenly madly in love... I'm gonna need a bit more development than that, y'all!

Also, notice in the above scenes that there isn't a whole lot of detail about what their mouths are doing. The sensory details are by no means limited to lips and tongues. Make the kiss a full-body experience. What's happening to your character's pulse? Their body temperature? What are their hands doing? What does the other character smell like when they're this close together? Make the kiss stop your reader's world as much as it stops your character's.

Can a kiss convey negative emotions? Absolutely! If someone's heart isn't in it, or they're repulsed by the other person, or their conscience is eating them alive about something, their kiss will almost certainly give that away. People can fake it, sure, but their mind and body will react in ways that they—and your reader, if we're in that character's POV—won't miss. Show us their apathy, their revulsion, or their guilt in the way their heart sinks, their stomach roils, or they can't quite get into the kiss. Raise that red flag for the other character to see or for them to obliviously overlook.

The sky is, as always, the limit!

To recap:

- Emotions, emotions, emotions!

- Don't focus exclusively on the mouth.
- Movies/TV are a great resource for what makes a kiss memorable and impactful.
- Significant kisses should follow and enhance the dynamic you've been building all along (unless you're intentionally shifting that dynamic by crossing that physical line).
- Kisses can convey negative emotions, too.

CHAPTER 4

YOU CAN TELL A LOT ABOUT A MAN BY THE WAY HE (UN)DRESSES

CLOTHING AND SEX SCENES

There are two facets to the discussion of clothes in sex scenes:

- How much clothing a person keeps on
- How they remove what they take off

What do I mean by this? Essentially, that sex while partially-dressed is a whole different vibe than naked sex. It can mean the characters are in a hurry—either they don't have much time or they simply can't wait. It can mean they're trying to stay warm or dry, or that they're just not in a place where they can get naked comfortably.

Similarly, *how* one removes clothes says a lot about the scene for the above reasons, and also about their mood, their need, etc. Sensually removing a partner's or one's own clothing one article at a time is very different from carelessly tossing things away or literally ripping something off.

Apparently when she'd kissed me in my office, she'd held back. Right now? She was not. She gripped my hair in one hand and had her other arm clamped around my waist, and she kissed me like a woman possessed. Deep and hard, breathless, and if this was even a hint of all the other things she could do with her mouth, I wasn't going to survive to see morning.

I reciprocated, too—squeezing her butt, sliding my hands up her chest, getting her damn jacket out of the way so I could really feel her breasts even if it was still through her blouse and bra. She gave a shrug and her jacket landed on the floor. It was probably expensive. Dry clean only and all that. If she cared, she didn't show it.

- BCC

And do be mindful when your characters start tearing clothes off. It can certainly be hot and sexy, but it can also give a literal bodice ripper vibe, not to mention some people just really don't find it hot to have their clothes torn. Like, I don't care how horny you are, my dude—that dress cost a fortune and so did the bra.

Of course you can still write it. Fantasy and all that. But you're not in quite the same hurry as your cloth-ripping character, so take the time and think about how it will land with readers, how the other character would actually feel about it, etc. Make sure your scene has the intended effect.

I've done this myself! This exchange would not have

worked in any of my other books, but with the antagonistic dynamic between these two, it *does* work here:

Ricardo fumbled with the top button on August's shirt. Then the second. His fingers didn't quite want to cooperate—not while his mouth was busy getting schooled by August's.

"This shirt is fucking expensive," August said against his lips. "You tear it, I swear to Christ I will—"

Ricardo had never before taken so much delight in yanking open a shirt and sending the buttons flying. And *nothing* had ever been more deeply satisfying than the way August gasped and froze, his expression a mix of horror, offense, and...oh, yeah, he was definitely turned on by it.

For a few seconds, they stared at each other in stunned silence, Ricardo still clutching the sides of August's open shirt as one of the buttons did a *click-rattle-rattle-rattle* across the kitchen floor before coming to a stop somewhere.

"I..." August stammered. "I can't believe..."

"Yeah?" Ricardo grinned, tugging August's shirt free from his trousers. "What are you gonna do?"

"You son of a bitch," August growled, and claimed a deep, bruising kiss. Ricardo pulled at the shirt again, snapping off the last two buttons, and August made a bitchy sound, but it was muffled by the kiss neither of them had broken. Between them, they pushed the shirt off August's shoulders, and it finally landed on the floor. Something clattered—a cufflink, Ricardo thought—but neither of them stopped to find out.

- Hitman vs. Hitman
Co-written with Cari Z

Context and intent matter, so just be sure your scene reads the way you want it to.

Also, as an aside, and this is more to filmmakers than writers:

Literally no one who wears glasses thinks it's sexy for someone to yank them off and throw them. *drops mic*

Anyway. For some scenes, peeling off each article of clothing is perfect. For others, it's way too slow. Just don't feel like you must pick one or the other, or even that your characters have to get fully naked before they do the deed.

Alyssa tore the wrapper with her teeth. Between them, they managed to get the condom rolled onto his cock. They didn't bother pushing his trousers off —they were far enough out of the way. Getting naked wasn't as important as getting him inside her, and he didn't resist at all when she pulled him down on top of her. She parted her legs for him, and as he guided himself to her, she was on the verge of losing her mind.

"Fuck me," she begged. "Please, fuck—"

"Don't mind if I do."

One thrust, and he was all the way inside her.

They both froze, lips almost touching, but neither of them moving or even breathing.

"Oh. My God." He brushed their lips together, then let his head fall beside hers. "You feel..." He withdrew slowly, pulling out maybe an inch, and then thrust again.

Alyssa yelped. She gripped his jacket just for something to hold on to, and rocked her hips as he picked up speed. She was completely naked, and he was still almost completely dressed, his warm tux and trousers brushing against her body with every thrust, and she'd never imagined that could be so fucking hot. His belt buckle marked time, jingling sharply every time he moved. He was dressed, and she was naked, and they were fucking, and she almost never came from this alone, but if he kept moving like that...

- I'll Show You Mine

Leaving some clothes on, especially while one person is fully or partially dressed, can create a lot of opportunity for sensory details. It can also, like many things, be used to show a changing dynamic or a juxtaposition to something from earlier in the story. As an example of both of these things, the first time Dom and Sergei fool around is while Dom is fully dressed and Sergei—a stripper—is completely naked and giving him a lap dance.

Later, we see them change things up:

"Take off your clothes." Sergei freed himself from Don's embrace and nodded toward the armchair beside the table. "Then sit."

"My clothes?"

"That's what I said, isn't it." Sergei still grinned, but in his eyes was the commanding, take-no-shit stripper who'd gotten in his face the same night he'd gotten on his lap. Oh hell yes.

Dom stripped, and then threw a towel on the chair since, well, God knew what else the furniture in here had been used for. As soon as he was seated, Sergei—fully dressed and visibly hard—straddled him, his shirt nearly touching Dom's face and his bulge grazing Dom's chest.

He started to reach for Sergei, but hesitated. "May I?"

"Yeah." Sergei leaned in closer, resting his hands on the back of the chair. "Please do."

Dom slid his hands up Sergei's chest, the fabric of his shirt pulling beneath his touch. This was even hotter than he'd anticipated. The juxtaposition—clothed stripper, naked customer—was a tease to end all teases. Though Dom could put his hands on him, he couldn't *touch* him, and it was Sergei's clothes, not his own, that kept their flesh from meeting. He could touch, but he couldn't feel. Not quite. Muscles moved beneath the surface, but the shirt tempered the heat of Sergei's skin.

- If The Seas Catch Fire

Basically, if characters are going to get intimate, chances are, some or all of the clothing is coming off. Don't overlook that opportunity to elevate your scene.

CHAPTER 5

OMG, I'M COMING... AGAIN? ALREADY?

For example, I've read scenes where a male character had an absolutely mind-blowing orgasm... then proceeded to rail the other character for ages until they too reached their climax.

While it's a hot fantasy, it's difficult not to think, "No, he most certainly did not."

Another issue with on-page orgasms is the ease with which characters can come. In reality, it's only relatively recently that we can talk openly about sex and sexual dysfunction enough for people to understand that orgasms can actually be quite difficult to achieve, especially clitoral/vaginal orgasms.

Orgasms as a result of vaginal penetration alone are as common in erotic fiction as people walking off gunshot wounds in action films, and they're about as realistic. The vast majority of people aren't going to keep fighting and running and throwing out witty catchphrases after taking a forty-five to the arm, and the vast majority of people being penetrated vaginally are going to need some additional stimulation to cross the finish line.

And so goes the delicate dance between "ooh, it would be so nice to have that happen for real" and "yeah, okay, *that* would never happen."

In reality, for some people, being on the receiving end of vaginal penetration is enough to bring them to orgasm, but in *many* cases, it's not. Similarly, prostate stimulation can be enough to cause an orgasm for some, while others can't even maintain an erection while being anally penetrated. None of this is a sign of someone lacking prowess in the bedroom —it's simply how the human body works. Additional stimulation is often needed—fingers, toys, etc.

Your character's ease at achieving orgasm is certainly up to you, but remember that if it's difficult for a character to climax, this is a perfect opportunity for their partner to shine. Or not, if that's what you're going for.

Let's say you have a character who is taking a long time to come. Here are a few ways their partner could respond:

- "I'll keep going as long as you want me to." *cue oral sex until their neck is stiff and their tongue cramps, but they're happy to keep going*
- "Well, I'm done, so I'm going to sleep."
- Ask for guidance and follow their partner's lead.
- Bring out a toy.
- Get frustrated because everyone else they've been with has gotten off this way, and make sure their partner knows how impatient they are.

Some of those scenarios are definitely not ideal, right? Total mood killers! But that's actually okay because as we discussed in another chapter, **not every sex scene has to have a positive outcome**. Characters can be interrupted, frustrated, upset, angry—remember that a sex scene can absolutely be a means by which you *complicate* things. It can create a reason for a character to grovel and redeem themself. Bringing some reality into play with orgasms definitely doesn't *have* to make your scene/story too real or boring!

There is also the matter of how a character and their equipment feel after an orgasm. Those in possession of a clitoris may look askance at your character continuing to go to town on the other character's clitoris immediately following an orgasm, without backing off or being gentle at all. If they have an amazing orgasm thanks to their partner's oral prowess, and that partner keeps right on going with their mouth, they're probably going to have to peel the recipient off the ceiling for an entirely different reason. Because there does come a point where "hypersensitive" translates to "OMFG that hurts."

Similarly, the be-penised will testify that their equipment can become uncomfortably sensitive following an orgasm.

The fact is, regardless of genitalia, there's a recovery period after an orgasm. The erection softens and most people are at least a little tired at this point. Drained, if you will. So this can quickly become one of those scenarios where it's very easy for the fantasy to tip into "reader crossing their legs uncomfortably" territory, which is *generally* not what we're going for with sex scenes.

Let your characters recharge. This also creates tons of opportunity for your characters to bond or wind each other up. Give them time to enjoy the afterglow. Let them catch their breath, maybe kiss and touch lazily, until they're both ready to go another round.

This doesn't mean everyone needs to take a twenty-minute break and ~~let the Zambonis run over the~~ oops, I write too much hockey. But you get what I'm saying. People can and do keep going after an orgasm.

Just maybe have the participants take their fingers off the trigger for a minute or two in between.

CHAPTER 6

DON'T EXAGGERATE THE SIZE OF YOUR FISH

I see this a lot. Breasts large enough they'd create balance issues in real life, not to mention massive neck and shoulder pain. Penile proportions that would make large livestock envious. While fantasy is certainly fun, it's very, very easy to tip over into cartoonish proportions.

First, let's talk physiology.

As I said, there's the issue of physically balancing with wildly disproportionate features, not to mention pain. I've heard those with smaller breasts insisting that the "big breasts are painful" notion is just something people with larger breasts say to… I don't know, make them feel like they're not missing out on anything. But as someone on the ouchy end of the boob size spectrum, I can say with some authority that there is absolutely some truth to it. There's a reason breast reductions can be and often are performed for the express purpose of minimizing pain. Which is to say, big breasts aren't all they're cracked up to be.

So if your character does have a pair on the larger side, this is fine, but you might get some raised eyebrows and winces from readers if your GGG character is astride their partner, bouncing away merrily without the slightest discomfort.

Also, implants usually feel different from natural breast tissue. There is usually some discreet but noticeable scarring, and the implant is usually harder and smoother than the existing tissue. There are variations to this, of course, based on physiology, healing, the skill of the surgeon, the type of implant, etc., but it's something to keep in mind if your character has implants.

While we're on the subject of large body parts, let's talk about the penis. According to the National Institute of Health, the average erect penis is between 5.1 and 5.5 inches[1]. According to Medical News Today, the average depth of the vagina is 3-7 inches[2]. So, at least when we're discussing penis-in-vagina intercourse, gigantic penises are, perhaps, somewhat impractical.

The main reason I point out these dimensions is because I can't count the number of times I've read a male character with an enormous penis—like, ten inches or more, described as such multiples times because, y'all, you *need to understand* he has a *huge schlong*—and then he's "burying it to the hilt" inside the heroine. Um... ouch? Especially when we're talking about the petite virgin heroine he's "taken with a single thrust"?

As always... fantasy vs. reality. There's nothing wrong with writing a character with a large penis. Just bear in mind what the picture you might be painting for the reader with the dimensions and the actions during a sex scene.

While we're on the subject of potential ouchies as a result of unusual dimensions, please, please, *please* realize that the penis *does not* penetrate the uterus. It doesn't go through the cervix at all. Not without requiring medical attention afterward, anyway, which is generally not considered pleasurable or sexy. And the penis really shouldn't hit the cervix very hard, either—pounding the cervix like a jackhammer is about as comfortable as slapping the testicles with a spatula. Unless you want to make the reader wince—and it's fine if that's what you're going for—keep that in mind.

Adonis vs. Average Joe

There is also the matter of what your reader wants. Again, fantasy. But more and more, especially in recent years, I've heard readers express that they *crave* normal bodies in their romance and erotic fiction.

I've spoken to women who feel ugly because all the heroines in romance are either skinny, tall, and giant-breasted or described as big beautiful women (BBWs). Even those who are described as plain are the equivalent of "nerdy girl" in a teenage movie who's actually beautiful beyond words + glasses. They wish there could be more women like them: average and imperfect.

Similarly, many men who read romance—gay or otherwise—have found themselves feeling unintentionally body-shamed or inadequate. Between the covers and descriptions, all the men in their books are over six foot, have effortlessly maintained six-packs, enormous penises, and their hairline hasn't moved since they were fifteen. After a while, this becomes a pattern that can leave a reader feeling less like they're reading about fantasy men and more like they, personally, will never be anyone's fantasy man.

Romance and erotica readers are voracious readers. They read enough to see these patterns, and many do start to get bummed out after a while when the pattern starts to be, "you aren't desirable enough to experience sex or love like this."

You can certainly write about Adonis, but Average Joe needs love, too, and you will endear yourself tremendously to your readers if you also present to them characters *like them* who are sexy and desired.

To recap:

- There's a very fine line between "that's hot" and "that hurts."
- It's very easy for fantasy proportions to reach cartoonish (and painful).
- Average Joe needs love, too.

CHAPTER 7

THE PACKAGE HAS BEEN DELIVERED

PENETRATION

Eons ago, on the seemed-funny-at-the-time-but-is-problematic-in-hindsight *Big Bang Theory*, Penny got blackout drunk and hooked up with Raj. All kinds of drama ensued for reasons, but later in the episode, Raj admitted that he came while putting on the condom. Penny is relieved to hear that they didn't actually have sex, and all is well going forward. And it wasn't because there was any concern about her getting pregnant—it just didn't actually count anymore because penetration didn't happen.

This always struck me as weird. I mean, they slept together. They were naked in bed together. Presumably they did things leading up to him putting on a condom.

But since penetration never occurred, Penny was enormously relieved. They didn't really have sex! Everything went back to normal after that because the issue was not that they got drunk, got naked, and fooled around. It was that—up until that moment—everyone thought penetration had occurred.

Kind of weird when you think about it, isn't it?

So that's what I want to touch on in this chapter. In

talking with writers about sex scenes, I've picked up a lot of frustration from people who can't make a particular scene work, or who can't figure out how to get their characters from Situation X to Penetration Y. They get so hung up on the need for a penetrative sex scene that they struggle to write the scene—or even the story—at all.

Spoiler: Penetration isn't required.

It still "counts" as a sex scene if there isn't penile penetration. It still counts as erotic if penetration never occurs in the entire story.

Because there is more to sex than penetration. I suspect a lot of people would be much happier if their partners understood that, and I think a lot of authors would feel less pressure to write their scenes/stories a certain way.

So I hereby give you, as an author who has written erotic fiction that didn't include anal or vaginal penetration, permission to write the smuttiest of smutty smut fic without ever putting a penis into an orifice.

I sound a bit snarky here, and I'm trying to keep it lighthearted, but there really does seem to be a ton of pressure to include specific types of sex in books. In stories that involve at least one penis, the rule seems to be that if a penis doesn't go into an orifice that isn't the mouth, then the sex scene doesn't count. Or that if at least one sex scene doesn't include such penetration, then the relationship hasn't been consummated. It's not *actually* sex.

The result is authors feeling pressured to include penile penetration even when it doesn't suit the story, the scene, etc. It can be incredibly obvious, too, when the author is clearly trying to make a penetrative sex scene happen just to check off that item on the list, rather than letting the characters engage in a way that fits organically with the story.

I wrote one book where both characters mention they enjoy anal sex, and that they're looking forward to engaging in it together. For various reasons, though, neither sex scene in the story ends up lending itself to anal play. So... it never happens. Both men are absolutely satisfied, and the sex scenes are (in my opinion) hot. They satisfy what I intended with the scenes—to show the characters getting intimate, and to get the reader hot under the collar. If I'd decided to (pardon the mental image) shoehorn some anal sex into the scene, it honestly would've ruined the vibe and probably left the reader with some questions about things like cleanup.

I mention this in another chapter, but I feel it's worth repeating here: my bestselling M/M romance *ever* contains zero penetrative sex. One of the characters tells the other early on that he doesn't enjoy anal sex, and that's that. The two still enjoy plenty of steamy sex scenes that leave both of them satisfied, but his boundary is firm, and it stays in place for the whole book.

Penetration is *not* required.

Which is more important—writing the best scene possible for those characters in that situation? Or making sure someone put a penis into an orifice?

This thought process can come in handy when dealing with characters who are injured/wounded, too. I've read some scenes where it would've been perfectly intimate and sexy if they'd just fooled around a little, but they ended up engaging in penetration anyway. And it's difficult to suspend my disbelief in those scenes when my mind is screaming:

· · ·

a. I don't think someone who's recently lost that much blood is going to be able to achieve, never mind maintain, an erection.

b. Yo, with that kind of injury, it hurts to get gently bumped. Thrust not, good sir.

c. Oh, that's gonna smart. Oh. Ow. OW!

d. There's gonna be some resuturing happening after this. Ow.

Sex is a physical act. Bodies get jarred. Jarred injuries *hurt*. I'll get into that more in a later chapter, but it underscores what I'm saying here, which is that penetration is not critical to every sex scene or every story. If you find yourself struggling to make a sex scene work, consider that you might be trying to force an element that just doesn't fit. Maybe they're not in a situation where penetrative sex is practical, comfortable, or even possible. Maybe it just isn't necessary at that stage of the story, even if it is the final sex scene.

Or maybe your characters just aren't into penetrative sex.

Write your characters, your scenes, and your stories the way they need to be written. If that means no penetration, then go forth and write them that way.

To recap...

- There is more to sex than penile penetration.
- Penile penetration is not necessary if it doesn't fit your story, your scene, or your characters.
- That whole Penny and Raj episode was ridiculous.

CHAPTER 8

YES OR NO?
CONSENT IN SEX SCENES

Trigger Warning: Discussions of rape and coercion.

Agency is hot. It's the 21st century, and no one should be ashamed of wanting sex or pursuing it. Your heroine being coy in the name of not appearing slutty, and your hero forcing himself on her because he knows she really wants it, and the heroine thinking to herself, "you know, I totally didn't say yes, but this is actually hot, so it's okay..." That's not hot anymore. In my opinion, it never was, but such was the 1980s.

Think I'm joking about the 1980s?

No. No, I'm not.

Part I
Rape in Erotic Fiction

First, we need to talk about dubcon, non-con, forced seduction, and rape. There is plenty of debate over whether rape fantasies are good, bad, cathartic, unhealthy, etc. That's not what this book is for, though. Fact is, rape fantasies exist, and they exist in some areas of erotica. Same with non-con and dubcon.

Remember how I said that this is the 21st century and consent is hot? That kind of implies that there was a time when it wasn't. Right?

Kind of, yeah. Because there was absolutely an era when consent was… optional at best.

Many years ago, back in that era of consent-ish romance, teenage me picked up a Regency romance. In it, the hero—and boy do I use that term loosely here—raped the heroine. This wasn't forced seduction (something I'll get into in this chapter). It was violent rape, and it was *meant* to be.

I was uncomfortable as hell, convinced this must be some kind of mistaken identity. I kept reading, certain we would discover that guy wasn't actually the hero, and the real hero would swoop in, stab him through the eyeballs, and be the man the now-traumatized heroine totally deserved.

I was right about the mistaken identity, but not in the way I'd hoped.

A few chapters later, we learn that the hero thought the heroine was someone else. I don't remember how he justified raping the woman he thought he'd raped, mostly because I was so horrified that this scene led into him and the heroine having sex. He even made some comment about "you're still a virgin, that didn't count" literally while he was getting physical with her.

To this day, I couldn't tell you the title of the book or the name of the author. It was also the reason I didn't touch another romance novel for years, and it's entirely possible it's the source of my aversion to Regency romances[1].

That's an example of obvious sexual assault. It wasn't even painted as such. And then there is the trope at the center of the 1980s' bodice rippers: "forced seduction," which was the era's answer to female sexual agency—if he forced herself on her and she secretly enjoyed it, then she could have hot and wild sex without being a dirty whore who *wants* hot and wild sex. For the younger folk, no, I'm really not joking.

And for the record, I'm not shaming authors for what they wrote or readers for what they read. My issue is with society and publishers of the time who made such a work-around necessary in the first place. Those books and their authors eventually paved the way to romance as we know it today. Romance novels have a long and strange history, particularly in the United States of Puritanism, and the very short and oversimplified summary is that the bodice rippers of yesterday are *part* of why we have the consensual steam and eroticism in our romances now.

In this day and age, erotic and romantic fiction can be a lot more unabashed. People—including those in possession of vaginas—can want it, pursue it, and have it. Consent is *in*.

But old habits die hard, and even without the "need" for forced seduction anymore, erotic fiction can toe—or cross— the line into sexual assault *without actually acknowledging it*. I can't count the number of times I've been blindsided by clear sexual assault in books that were not labeled as dubcon, non-con, forced seduction, or rape fiction. They were meant to be hot and titillating, and the scenes *were not acknowledged as rape*. In fact, they were intended to be romantic and sexy.

Yeah, I'm generally of the belief that writers should be

free to write anything they want. And in this area, that holds. But the hill I will die on a thousand times over is that sexual assault should be labeled as such. If you want to write sex scenes without consent—go for it. Just... please... call them what they are. By all means, give readers of non-con and dubcon what they want... but put up a road sign so those who don't enjoy it—and can indeed be traumatized by it—can steer clear.

Also I'm not going to call out any books by name because lawyers are expensive, but adding leather to a rape scene doesn't make it BDSM. It makes it a rape scene with leather.

As you can see, this is a hot topic. In the realms of erotic fiction, I would argue that few things are more hotly debated than consent. The reason I'm going into detail about it is that there are few things worse—and quite possibly traumatic for someone who's experienced sexual assault firsthand—than reading a sex scene, realizing it's actually rape, and the author expecting you to think it's hot and sexy. When a scene is clearly a form of sexual assault, and it's treated as romantic, that is liable to put me off an author forever.

As I said before, you can write anything you want. Just be aware of how your characters' actions will alter how they're perceived by your readers.

So let's talk about forced seduction for a minute. Forced seduction—the primary heat source in bodice rippers—comes from an era when sexual agency was not a thing a respectable woman was supposed to have, never mind act upon. The only way to have the sexy, passionate scenes readers wanted was to frame those scenes in a way that kept the woman respectable. She wasn't seeking out the sex. The sex happened to her. And since the man was hot and bold—

the alpha male that has been a staple of romance for decades—the woman actually enjoyed it. Just like he knew she would.

Grossed out yet? Yeah, me too.

In essence, it was a form of slut-shaming. A woman could only enjoy acts of wanton lust as an afterthought—enjoying something being done to her regardless of her desires, enjoyment, and consent. In other words, a scene of forced seduction was less shameful than a woman having and exercising sexual agency.

Those days are behind us now. Like I said before, it's the 21st century. No one should be ashamed of wanting sex or pursuing it. And yes, you can absolutely create sexual tension while still giving your characters agency. After all, agency includes the ability to say yes.

From a purely personal standpoint, I don't like erotic fiction where consent isn't clear. Unless the character is a literal mind reader, there is no way to know for sure that the other character's resistance is merely hiding the fact that they actually do want it. And even if the character *is* a mind reader, they'd still better hold out for a yes, or else they're dead to me.

But that's me. I'm not every reader, and I might not be your target audience. Really the only reason I'm even pointing this out here is not to kink shame or to tell people what they should and shouldn't read. It's simply to express why I think this particular trope should be *clearly marked*. I'm absolutely not here to tell you that you can't or shouldn't write erotic fiction with dubious or non-existent consent. In fact, there is plenty of debate over whether rape fantasies are good, bad, cathartic, unhealthy, etc., and that's not what this book is for.

Moving forward with this chapter on consent, I'm going

to assume that we're discussing scenes that are *not* non-con or dubcon, and advise accordingly.

Part II
Affirmative consent

Written well, affirmative consent is *hot*.

No, your characters don't need to fill out forms and have them carbon-copied and notarized. Your character doesn't need to explicitly say "I hereby consent to you touching my person, including but not limited to playing with nipples, stroking my genitals, and inserting one or more lubricated fingers into my butthole." I mean, that's totally fine if that's what your characters *want* to do, but you know what I mean.

And yes, you can absolutely create sexual tension and turn up the heat on a scene while still giving your characters agency. After all, there are endless ways to request or give consent in hot, sexy ways.

Austin spoke, low and rumbly: "You are so sexy like this."

I barely kept a whimper from escaping my lips. "Am... Am I?"

"Uh-huh." He leaned in closer. "May I kiss you, Levi?"

Now it was beyond surreal. This man who had me at a total physical disadvantage... was asking permission for something as simple as a kiss? He could have taken it. Claimed it. Claimed *me*.

But not without my consent.

So much hung in the air between us as he waited for my response, and I kind of wanted to get drunk on that holding-on-by-our-fingernails feeling. On that exhilarating moment of standing in the open door of the plane, about to jump. He was offering me so much that I hadn't even imagined before yesterday, and I was rock-hard and trembling and eager for everything that waited on the other side of "*Yes.*"

My hunger for him had to be written all over my face by now, but he didn't move. He took nothing. He waited for the explicit invitation as if I still had the faculties for English.

I swallowed. Swept my tongue across my lips. And finally, by some miracle, I whispered a shaky, "*Please.*"

- The Right to Remain

Get creative! Have one character whisper to the other what they want to do, followed by, "Would you like that?"

In another example, Anna Zabo's Max and Tom navigate consent and establish one of Tom's serious limits, all without losing the sexiness of the moment:

Slowly Max pressed a hand to Tom's chest, over his heart. "Before we go any further, I need you to understand something, Tom."

"Yeah?" His heart was beating so fast.

"You can always say no or tell me to stop.

Anytime, for any reason. I won't get angry. I won't be upset. I may worry, but that's because I don't want to harm you. Do you understand?"

Wonder opened up in Tom. Also something sharp, like the pull of an old wound. "I—yeah. I'll tell you."

"Good." Max traced his hand up, skimming Tom's jaw before cupping the back of his neck. "May I kiss you?"

"Oh fuck, yes." It burst out of Tom, and before he could say anything else, Max had his mouth and Tom was moaning and opening against lips and tongue. No space separated them now. Max's weight, his hard body, crushed Tom into the unyielding wall.

The kiss was masterful, dominating, and everything Tom had hoped for. He gripped Max's coat, needing to be stripped and flogged and fucked with the same commanding presence.

When Max finally relented and opened up space, he was smiling, and breathless. "Well, you're going to be fun." Super-sexy voice, all dark and passion.

"Just don't ask me to kneel."

Max cupped his face. "I don't need you to kneel." Those words were dark, as well. "I won't ask you for that."

- Cinnamon Roll
Anna Zabo

Consent *is* sexy.

Make it a game. Make your character explicitly ask for what they want. Make them spell out to their partner what they want to do to them until their partner is ready to come unglued. The sky really is the limit here... and the same applies to the ways a reader might interpret (correctly or not) a scene as *lacking* consent.

For example, if the characters are getting rough, and one person throws the other down, pins them, and forces penetration—is the pinned character into it? Or is this going too far?

It doesn't take much to make it clear. A single line about a flutter of panic will cast the scene into a very different light than a rush of anticipation and excitement.

Again, this circles back to intent. How do you want your character to feel during the scene? Arguably more important, how do you want your *reader* to feel during the scene? What do you want them focusing on?

Do you *want* your reader to stop and wonder if the character really wants what's happening? It's okay if you answer yes to this as long as you're cognizant that that's what you're doing. If you answer no, then it's up to you to make sure consent is clear.

I've read scenes that were supposed to be hot and titillating, but I spent most of the scene cringing because I couldn't decide if the non-POV character was actually *into* it. And if they were, how the POV character knew. Maybe they knew, but I sure didn't.

If that's the effect you're going for, then fine.

But if you don't want your reader worrying if the scene is consensual, then it's up to you as a writer to make it clear that everyone involved is onboard.

And now I get to call upon my experience as a porn editor for something useful.

When I was working on one particular scene, the actors did an interview beforehand where they talked about their everyday sex life (they were an actual couple). At one point, the man made a comment about giving the woman a particular drug while they were having sex. She giggled a bit, but said nothing.

That point in the interview made me uncomfortable because the way he worded it, it sounded like he'd slipped her the drug or told her to take something without telling her what it was. If I recall, he'd asked her to lick his fingers, and he had the drug on his fingers.

I didn't feel comfortable, so I asked the director about it, and he assured me that it had been a consensual thing. Though they hadn't made it clear during the interview, other conversations and off-camera comments assured him that the woman had been an aware and willing participant. This was a relief, but in the end I still left the comments out of the interview, because the *viewer* wouldn't have the necessary additional context.

You, the author, are the director. You're privy to the conversations that don't make it onto the screen. The reader is not.

So how explicit do your characters need to be about asking for and giving? Well, that's up to you. It depends largely upon your story, your characters, context, etc.

Maybe your characters are completely new to each other. They might need to ask outright for consent more than a pair who's been together long enough to read each other. Body language is sometimes enough. Non-verbal communication can be more than sufficient *as long as your reader understands it* as clearly as your characters do.

To recap:

- To write rape fantasies or not is your decision. But readers who don't like them will appreciate knowing that's what it is before they start reading.
- It can be argued that bodice rippers had their place in the 1980s, but there is no longer a need to hide female sexual desire behind sexual assault.
- Affirmative consent is as sexy as you want it to be.

CHAPTER 9

OH, THE PAIN

BUMPS, BRUISES, BULLETS, & BOINKING

If you're writing erotic suspense or something involving military characters, athletes, or anyone else who's been through the physical wringer, this chapter probably pertains to you. We're going to talk about sex scenes when your characters are beaten, battered, and bruised.

Let's face it, y'all—sex is a strenuous physical activity. And as anyone who watches professional sports can attest, an injury can derail a strenuous physical activity in a hurry. I'm going to go out on a limb and guess that a football player carted off during the third quarter probably isn't getting frisky later that night. Even if they are, I'd bet a couple of doughnuts that they're doing it a little more gingerly than usual.

Injuries cause pain. Pain affects sex.

I know, that seems obvious, but fiction does seem to be a realm in which someone can be on Death's door and still be up for a rough quickie. The last thing you want during a passionate sex scene, though, is for your reader to be grimacing and side-eyeing their ereader while thinking, "*After what they've been through, that's* gotta *hurt.*" If your reader is spending the whole scene worrying about the character's back injury or if those stitches are going to hold, then your scene *probably* isn't accomplishing what it's supposed to.

Now, characters can absolutely have sex while they're battered and bruised. The key is taking their injuries into consideration. Did your character hurt their knee? Maybe don't have them kneeling and thrusting. Has it only been a few hours since a nasty fender bender that gave them some awful whiplash? Probably not the best time to give a marathon session of cunnilingus. Were they in a nasty brawl that would make an MMA fighter wince? It might not hurt to hold off on anything overly athletic until they've at the very least spent some time with an icepack.

The body does heal, and it can bounce back remarkably quickly from some pretty serious trauma, but pain is a thing.

Car crashes hurt. Even a relatively low speed, low impact car accident is enough to jar someone, and that soreness is a real mood killer.

Getting thrown from a horse hurts. If you've never been involuntarily dismounted from a 1,500 lb. animal with an overactive prey instinct, please let me be the first to tell you that even if you land in a cushy pile of leaves... it still hurts. The harder the surface, the faster the horse is moving, the more violently you're thrown—the more it hurts. That pain is not sexy. Ask me how I know.

As Landon unlaced his boots, he looked up at me.
"I'm going to guess the 'not fooling around tonight' thing still stands."

I coughed a laugh, wincing as I shrugged off my

jacket. "I mean, we *can*, but there won't be a lot of excitement."

He chuckled, stood, and toed off his boots. As he nudged them up against the row of shoes, he said, "Nah. I know some people are into pain, but I don't think anyone is into *that* kind of pain."

"God, I hope not. I mean, I'm not one to kink shame, but if you need a horse falling on top of you..." I trailed off into a grimace.

- Underdog

When you start getting into higher intensity injuries, the pain and immobility are going to escalate too. I'm not going to derail this chapter into all the things Hollywood has lied to you about when it comes to firearms, but I will say this: bullet holes do a *lot* of damage. Hollywood has convinced us all that a small caliber through-and-through is little more than a flesh wound. Which, I mean, it *is* a flesh wound—a deep, nasty flesh wound that will take months to heal and might do some serious damage to muscles, tendons, ligaments, nerves, organs, and whatever else is in the way. A .22 caliber bullet leaves a deceptively small entrance wound, but it makes a *mess* once it starts ricocheting off bones. Imagine the board game Operation as a high-speed pinball machine, and you're close.

Then there's the exit wound. Even if the bullet goes in cleanly, it's not going to be as kind on the way out.

And that's before we start getting into shotgun slugs and larger caliber bullets.

The point of all this is quite simply: bullet holes are *major injuries.*

They do major damage. The blood loss alone is going to weaken a person, and absolute best-case scenario, they're going to be *sore*.

If your character has been close enough to an explosion to be burned or fragged, they're probably not going to be in the mood for much. The psychological trauma alone is quite likely going to bench their sex drive for a little. If they were close enough to the blast to be knocked off their feet, knocked unconscious, etc., then they're going to be in a world of hurt. As a reader, I can almost guarantee you that, with very few exceptions, if your character is having wild sex twenty-four hours after being thrown by an explosion, I will be side-eying you *so hard*. The concussion alone is going to do some serious physical trauma.

Speaking of concussions...

Concussions are unpleasant. Much like the fun experience of being thrown like a ragdoll off a horse... ask me how I know. In fact, that's how I got one of my concussions. Kind of a two-for-one when researching this book, but I digress. Even a relatively mild concussion is a *miserable* experience. When you get your bell rung, it sucks. It can screw with your balance, your ability to think coherently, your speech, and your memory. That alone is disconcerting enough to make sex unappealing. Throw in the headache, nausea, dizziness, and any bumps the impact might've left on your head, plus whatever other injuries you might've picked up, and seriously—sex is no bueno.

So am I saying you can't or shouldn't write sex scenes with injured characters? Of course not! But when a character is seriously knocked around, especially if there's a bullet hole or two, and then in the very next chapter he's having wild, acrobatic sex as if everything is fine...

I mean, we're back to that issue of some readers not

noticing or caring, but those who *do* notice and care will be yanked right out of the story. Personally, I'm in the latter category, and this is one of those things that can kill a scene or even an entire story for me.

That, and I'm of the belief that writing a "regular" sex scene with an injured character is essentially squandering an opportunity for something much more significant emotionally. There's an entire chapter in this book devoted to failed sex scenes, and this can definitely include situations where the mind is willing but the body is busted up.

It doesn't have to be a failed sex scene, either. Your characters can absolutely have satisfying sex to completion while one or both are injured (depending on the injury, of course). The question is how much should the injury affect the scene? And how should it affect it?

Maybe your characters are having "oh my God I thought I'd lost you" sex. Or "we're probably going to die after this, so to hell with it" sex. Or "this is the only thing that feels good right now" sex. Maybe they're both frustrated that they can't be as wild and rough as usual. Make that frustration palpable on the page—the desire for more combined with the tenuous restraint to keep from causing pain.

All of that is fine! The sex just isn't likely to be the same kind of athletic, bendy sex they'd have on a good day. But it can be emotionally charged in ways it wouldn't otherwise be. If it really is the best thing for your characters and your story to have a sex scene at that point, with injuries, then by all means write it. Just don't ignore an otherwise significant injury and waste an opportunity to write something that hits your reader in the feels.

Acute injuries aren't the only thing that can rein in a character's ability and desire to have sex. Chronic illnesses and injuries can absolutely have an affect on a character's sex life. But they don't have to be the *end* of the character's sex life. It just probably requires some modification in the short or long term, if only to avoid your reader screaming *"no way in hell are they doing that when they can barely turn their head!"* at their ereader.

Whether we're talking about chronic or acute pain, letting physical injuries and limitations curtail physical activities doesn't mean the scene has to be any less sexy than if they were pulling out all the stops. I have a few books featuring characters with chronic pain, and the sex scenes, while modified to minimize pain, still function the same as any other sex scene. They don't turn clinical or become less erotic just because there are limitations.

In this scene, one of my characters has chronic back pain after ejecting from a fighter jet, so sex is necessarily limited.

"Is your back all right, though?"

"Mm-hmm." He kissed under my jaw. "It's good. Maybe we should take advantage of it while it's not throwing a fit."

I shivered, arching under him, and ran my nails down his waist. "Anything you want. I'm all yours."

"Good," he moaned against my throat. "Because I want you so bad right now." He pushed himself up and looked in my eyes. "Seriously, anything you want tonight." He swept his tongue across his lips. "We can even fuck. If...if you want—"

"All I want is you."

"But if—"

I kissed him. "I want you," I whispered. "No

way in hell are we doing something that'll hurt you." And before he could protest, I claimed another long kiss, and his body relaxed against mine.

I pushed him onto his side, and he grunted softly when I wrapped my fingers around his cock. He did the same to me, blanking my brain and sending goose bumps up my spine.

It didn't matter that we couldn't fuck. I enjoyed some wild, headboard-pounding fucking as much as the next man, but this was amazing. Lying here, stroking each other and kissing, in no hurry at all but already out of breath—it didn't get any better than this.

And what kind of man would I have been if I'd taken him up on his offer, knowing how much pain he could very well be in afterward? No way was I making him spend a night in more pain because of me. I couldn't imagine hurting him.

So we stayed like that—legs intertwined under the sheet, hands moving in unison, lips moving lazily together. Little by little, the intensity grew. Grips tightened. Strokes picked up speed. Kisses were more frantic, more breathless. His skin was hot against mine, his breath cool as it rushed across my skin. He hooked a leg over mine. I held on to his shoulder with my free hand.

I wasn't in any hurry, but I sure as hell wasn't putting on the brakes either.

- Afraid to Fly

Just because there's significant pain involved—and even when the characters are consciously acknowledging it and trying not to make it worse—doesn't mean the scene can't still be hot, sexy, and satisfying for your characters and your reader.

This principle extends to characters with disabilities beyond chronic pain, too. An entire book could be written about this alone, but that is beyond the scope of my expertise, and is better left in the hands of someone with more knowledge on the subject. What I can say is that every disability is different, and every disabled person is different, so it is up to you to do your homework and determine how sex with this individual would be different. Read up on how a person with that disability might engage in sex; there are articles, blogs, Reddit posts, videos, etc., out there on exactly that.

Basically, don't forget that the pain or physical limitations are there. It's no longer a sex scene between your two characters—it's a threesome with both of them *and* the pain.

And few things will launch a reader out of the scene like a character swinging from the chandeliers three hours after leaving the hospital with a freshly stitched bullet hole.

To recap:

- Injuries hurt.
- Sex with injuries is doable, but the injuries are still there.
- Take advantage of the pain and vulnerability to deepen the emotions between your characters.
- Horses are jerks.

CHAPTER 10

LIKE A VIRGIN…
BECAUSE THEY ARE A VIRGIN.

Virgins. Let's talk about virgins. They're a popular trope in romance. What's not to love about sexual exploration, especially through the eyes of someone who's experiencing it all for the very first time?

To start with, there's the matter of what virginity means, since it's a pretty subjective thing. With straight people, it's generally accepted that penis-in-vagina sex is the point at which virginity is lost. Some will argue that anal sex doesn't count, or that oral doesn't count, and that generally speaking, that's the line in the sand.

But not everyone is heterosexual, and not every sexual encounter involves a penis and a vagina, and not everyone who engages in sex chooses to have penetrative sex. Different communities and different individuals have different definitions for where the line is and what does or doesn't count. With gay men, for example, do you define a man as having lost his virginity the first time he sucks cock? Has his cock sucked? Tops? Bottoms? The line isn't quite as clear, though *most* of the gay men I've talked to about this subject tend to agree that the rite of passage is giving oral sex.

I point this out because it's easy to fall into the heteronormative assumption that virginity is based on either penetrating or being penetrated with a penis. Since this is subject to some debate within the gay community, I tend to be specific about how the individual character defines it for himself, rather than implying that there is a universally accepted definition for all gay men.

Most of my characters are more concerned about their lack of experience (e.g., if other men will reject them or make fun of them, if they'll be able to satisfy other men, etc.) or whether they'll enjoy something (e.g., being penetrated anally might make someone nervous because he's concerned about pain, or he's not sure how he feels about giving oral sex). So the defining issue for them is less about a rite of passage and more about experiencing something new, exploring their curiosity, and overcoming their fears.

It's a good idea to decide where your characters stand with regard to this, and what the prevailing thoughts on the subject are within that character's community, rather than defaulting to heteronormativity. You don't need to turn your book into a thesis on what does or doesn't qualify as losing one's virginity. Just understand where your characters stand on it. What rite of passage is important to them? What activities excite or intimidate them?

Going forward in this chapter, for the sake of brevity, I'm going to use "virgin" as an all-encompassing term for a character who's sexually inexperienced. How inexperienced are they? That, of course, depends. You need to decide just how much of a virgin your character really is. Have they ever had any intimate contact at all? A person who's got a fair amount of experience with oral and even anal sex, but never vaginal, might still technically be considered a virgin, but they're going to have a substantially different perspective than someone who's never even been kissed.

Also, their partner's level of experience is going to make a difference. Are *both* characters virgins? Are they both completely inexperienced? Does one have more experience than the other, but still hasn't engaged in a particular activity? This will greatly shape the dynamic between your characters, so make sure you give it some serious thought ahead of time.

On this note, it's also important to understand *why* your character is a virgin. The answer can be as simple as "they hadn't met someone they wanted to have sex with." It doesn't have to be because of anything negative. But there are myriad other reasons why someone might still be a virgin at whatever stage in life. An oppressive upbringing. Trauma. Fear. Shyness. Religious or cultural reasons. Health issues. Personal preference. Asexuality (which might mean they're willing to have sex, and they enjoy it once they do, but they've never had any particular desire to do so). Even if it doesn't end up being something that you explore on-page, it is important for the author to understand it as a means of further understanding your character.

Expanding on this, take some time to consider how much your virgin knows about sex. Are they hyper-repressed thanks to their upbringing or culture? Do they masturbate regularly? Do they watch porn? Have they ever experienced an orgasm? Because your incredibly naïve and repressed virgin is probably not going to suck cock like a pro and might not realize anal sex exists, never mind that lube is necessary. By contrast, your porn-watching virgin who owns stock in Jergens and Kleenex is likely not going to be mystified by fellatio or startled to discover people sometimes put toys or penises into vaginas or anuses.

Similarly, if a character has been raised to think sex is dirty—in general, specific acts, specific gender pairings, etc.—then they may experience some emotional conflict during a sex scene. For example, take someone who was taught that anything other than vaginal sex is dirty and disgusting. Then, while in bed with the other character, they discover that receiving oral sex is *amazing*... but that pleasure might very well take a turn into shame, guilt, and even anger at their partner.

Remember that a lot of people have very complicated relationships with sex, and this can absolutely affect their ability to enjoy it. Those complex feelings can rear their heads during the act or after, and how your characters ride it out can make a tremendous difference in their personal development, their relationship arc, and their future sex scenes. That kind of experience certainly isn't universal, but it's important to understand how a new sexual experience will affect your character mentally and emotionally.

It's also good to keep in mind whether this is your virgin's first time being naked in front of someone else—at all, or in an intimate setting. For example, a hockey player, who has likely been desensitized to his and others' nudity in locker rooms all his life may very well get shy and self-conscious in the bedroom. Intimacy changes everything.

As an aside, a lot of these principles apply to someone engaging in a new *type* of sex or intimacy. Someone who's had sex with dozens of women could understandably be very nervous when they go to kiss a man for the first time. A person who's engaged in vanilla sex could quite possibly be overwhelmed at the prospect of a threesome or a BDSM scene. Be cognizant of how a new experience can and will affect your character, and embrace that in your sex scenes.

Does it hurt?

Well now that's a complicated question. Let's talk about pain.

It's pretty much accepted that when it comes to penetrative sex (vaginal or anal), the first time is going to hurt for the person on the bottom. And sometimes it does. But does it have to?

Here's the thing:

First time vaginal doesn't have to hurt, but it might.

First time anal might hurt, but it shouldn't.

With vaginal, the factors a person can't really control have to do with the hymen. That's just anatomy, and people have to work with what they have. What *can* be controlled are lubrication and relaxation, which are also factors that can be controlled for anal sex. The person on top can be patient and gentle, making sure the bottom is ready to be comfortably penetrated. Can there still be some pain or discomfort? Yes, but it's not universal, and a caring partner will take the time to make the experience as enjoyable and comfortable as possible.

Which is to say, if you want to write a deflowering scene where the person being penetrated enjoys it, there's nothing wrong with that. Maybe not "taking her with a single, deep thrust of his twelve-inch cock", though, you know? Give the top the opportunity to show how much they care about the person they're about to penetrate.

Also, tops can be inexperienced, too. They can go too fast, and they can inadvertently cause their partner pain. Does every top get overexcited, thrust in too fast, and come too soon? No. Those are certainly things that can happen, but they're not required. It's also entirely plausible for your inexperienced top to be so nervous, they can't get or maintain an erection.

You, the writer, can make this work for their character development and relationship evolution if it's appropriate for your story and characters.

If your virgin is being penetrated vaginally for the first time, it *might* hurt. It's a myth that the first time automatically results in pain and bleeding. Sometimes those can happen. When they do, it can be because of anatomy—not all hymens are the same—or because the penetrator dropped the ball and didn't warm up the oven first. If you just jam it in there without so much as a "well, hello," it's gonna smart.

With anal, there's no hymen, so that's a non-issue. And again, the first time doesn't *have* to hurt. It depends very much on how relaxed the recipient is, how patient the penetrator is, and how much lube is involved. The top's experience makes a difference, too; a patient, experienced, and conscientious top can make the bottom's first time pain-free or close to it.

By contrast, if your character is bottoming for the first time, and the top goes for broke, your readers are going to be squirming in their seats... and probably not the way you want them to be.

So how much should it hurt your character? Well, that depends on what you're going for. When your penis- or toy-wielding character goes in for the first time, do you want your reader to wince? Or do you want them to be aroused? Do you want it to be a perfect experience or a difficult one?

Don't take any of this to mean that a painful deflowering can't make for a hot or even poignant scene. It can be a moment for the other character to realize they need to be sensitive to the virgin's needs. It can be a clumsy moment. A tender one. A setback for their relationship, or a moment for them to strengthen their bond and deepen their trust. It's an opportunity for the top to comfort the bottom, ease their pain, or say or do the wrong thing and have to grovel or otherwise redeem themself.

The possibilities are infinite. Just don't assume that your virgin *must* be clueless, scared, awkward, and in pain, or that your top (virgin or otherwise) *needs* to be flawless. They can be if that's what fits your story, but it's not required.

Let people make mistakes, especially if it's their first time.

To sum it up...

- First time vaginal sometimes hurts, but it doesn't always.
- First time anal sometimes hurts, but it shouldn't.
- Understand why your character is a virgin and how that affects them mentally and emotionally going into a sex scene.
- Deflowering scenes are not required to have a clueless, terrified virgin or a supremely confident and experienced Dom.

CHAPTER 11

I WANT SEXY, NOT SEX ED
CONDOMS

Part I
Should My Characters Use Condoms?

In discussions with both readers and writers about the use of condoms in sex scenes, there is no shortage of controversy.

There are those who believe fiction should be fantasy at its fullest, without concerns about STIs or pregnancy. It's not meant to be a how-to guide for people. Condoms simply don't belong.

And there are those who find the lack of condoms to be uncomfortable and unsettling; in an era when there is so much talk about safe sex, some readers and writers alike can't get into the fantasy when characters don't take basic precautions.

In essence, it often comes down to:

"I don't want the scene ruined because I'm worried they're going to get pregnant or sick."

—versus—

"If I wanted to read about condoms, I'd pick up a sex ed book."

So what's the right answer?

As with most things, it ultimately comes down to the writer's discretion. I'm not going to tell you that your characters absolutely must use or even mention condoms. I will, however, say that I think the wise writer at least spends a little time thinking about the subject and making a conscious decision one way or another.

Before we go on, I should note that this conversation mostly applies to contemporary books. Science fiction and fantasy are entirely different animals. Historical really depends on how aware your characters would be of risks and available prophylactics/birth control. Other genres and subgenres may have different things to consider. So if this chapter doesn't really apply to what you're writing, then don't sweat it.

Also, the fact of the matter is that not everyone uses condoms. There are other methods of birth control, and things like PrEP for preventing HIV. And some people just... don't use condoms. There has been particular controversy within the M/M romance genre about the use of condoms and whether it reflects reality. To require that all gay male characters use them across the board is to erase the fact that, in life, not all gay men use them.

My stance is that the *author* should be aware of why their characters choose not to use them, even if the reason is as simple as "These characters don't use condoms." It may never need to be acknowledged or discussed on-page because, if these characters were real people, they wouldn't discuss it or even think about it. As with most things, it all boils down to the author being conscious of who their characters are, what's true to those characters, and how much of that needs to be on the page.

Will all readers respond positively to your characters using or not using condoms? No. You can't and won't please everyone. The best you can do—the thing I recommend most strongly with regard to every facet of a sex scene, and indeed with writing in general—is to be true to your characters and to your story.

All of that being said, this is a chapter about the use or absence of condoms in scenes. As such, I'm going to proceed from here talking about how to write their presence or absence, which means discussing this with the assumption that we're talking about characters who *would* either use or consider using them. If that doesn't apply to your character(s), this isn't meant to erase them or invalidate them (or you!)—just focusing on the subset to whom it *does* apply.

So with that in mind... how does one include or discuss condoms without killing the mood?

Condoms (and conversations about condoms) can be incorporated into a scene with a deft hand. They can be mentioned in passing so subtly that the reader only just registers their existence without actually stopping to think about it. Characters can quickly decide whether or not to use them with only a few lines of dialogue. Condoms need not slow down, interrupt, or ruin a sex scene any more than they do in real life (and if they do in real life... well... that's a whole other book about techniques that could use some work).

Let's start with conversations.

Part II
Discussing Condom Use

Personally, I default toward my characters using condoms. That doesn't mean they *all* use them, though. Simply put, my characters use condoms unless they have a reason not to, and that reason is always acknowledged on-page. Those who do use condoms just do so without any discussion or fanfare (unless those specific characters would discuss it).

Those who don't use them will, context permitting, talk about it. This doesn't mean they have to have lengthy discussions wherein they cite research and statistics. It is reasonable to assume that adult characters are aware of STI and pregnancy risks and prevention, and I'll just go with a brief conversation to make sure they're on the same page.

In one of my upcoming heterosexual romances, *When Yvette Moved In*, both characters are recently divorced because their spouses wanted children and they didn't. This is their entire discussion about condoms:

Brandon bit his lip and squirmed like he was holding back a shudder, and he met my gaze, his eyes gleaming with lust. "Before we go too far, though..." He glanced around. "I, um, don't suppose you have any condoms? Because I don't."

"In my room, yeah, but..." I licked my lips. "Look, I haven't been with anyone but my ex in years, and I have an IUD." I paused. "And I really do have it in, I promise. Because I don't want babies. *Ever*."

He chuckled. "It's okay, I believe you." Sobering, he held my gaze. "I haven't been with anyone but my ex, either. So I guess... in theory..."

"We could probably skip the condoms?"

We locked eyes. It was a risk, yes, but this

wasn't some random dude I'd picked up for a one night stand. This was *Brandon*, for God's sake.

"I totally get if you don't want to skip them," I said. "After everything..."

He chewed his lip, but then he shook his head and pulled me closer again. "We're good."

"You sure?"

"Definitely. You?"

I nodded. "Yeah."

We both grinned, and then Brandon kissed me again. Anticipation zinged through me. I wanted him so bad I couldn't see straight, and we may as well have just said out loud "we're about to fuck." Yes, please?

- When Yvette Moved In

At 221 words, this is probably on the long end of conversations I write to this effect. They cover their bases, mutually agree to skip condoms, and continue without the mood faltering in the slightest.

In Jordan Castillo Price's *Criss Cross*, Vic and Jacob have been dancing around penetrative sex since the previous book.

"Come on," I prompted. Just me, Jacob, and some body wash. Because all the talk about not having any condoms around had only been an excuse. We get blood tests quarterly on the force; all the cops do, even the elite ones like us. I'd just been a little leery about letting him in. Figuratively and literally.

- Criss Cross
PsyCop 2 by Jordan Castillo Price

57 words, and the condom issue is resolved. For that matter, it's resolved in a way that makes the scene hotter and more meaningful.

It can even be a little nihilistic. Say, when a couple of assassins in a life-or-death situation are seizing an opportunity to fool around:

August sat up and held out the lube.

Ricardo took it. "Condoms?"

"You think we're going to live long enough to worry about it?"

He had a point. Ricardo uncapped the lube, and as he stroked it on himself, he nodded toward the pillows. "Turn over. On your stomach."

- Hitman vs. Hitman
Written with Cari Z

Bottom line? Discussing whether to use condoms doesn't have to be a mood killer. If you find that it is killing the mood in your scene, rethink how your characters are approaching it. It could be a sign that they still have some ground to cover before they get into bed, or it could just be that the conversation needs to be written differently.

Part III

How to Use Condoms in a Scene
Without Killing the Scene

One argument I've often heard against including condoms is that they dampen the mood of the scene or ruin the fantasy. And they certainly can. Anything can!

Whether a condom ruins the mood or makes the scene simply depends on how it's written.

For example, there's no reason a condom can't be unobtrusive in a sex scene—existing and acknowledged, but as set dressing more than anything.

I was so tempted to shove him up against this wall and fuck him into oblivion, but the lust and need in his eyes—I wasn't about to miss that. Not a second of it.

So instead, I manhandled him around, guided him into the bathroom, and bent him over the counter roughly enough to drive a grunt out of him. "Get those pants off."

He didn't need to be told twice. Resting on one forearm, he undid his pants with the other while I fumbled with my own. By the time I'd rolled on the condom, we were the very picture of heat-of-the-moment hunger. Rumpled, half-buttoned shirts. Pants around our ankles. Ties hanging around our shoulders.

"Isaac." He fidgeted, rocking back against me like he was searching for my cock. "Please."

- Rookie Mistake

Written with Anna Zabo

Or it can be a more obvious prop, used in a way that intensifies the scene.

Though Jude's hands were usually rock steady, they were trembling as he tore the wrapper. A.J. hadn't been fucked in a long time, but at this point, he couldn't think of anything he wouldn't let Jude do. As long as they were fucking soon, he didn't care whose cock was in whose ass.

Just... now... please...

Jude moved closer, and when he rolled the condom over A.J.'s cock instead of his own, A.J. thought he was going to black out. *Yes. Oh God, yes.*

-Running With Scissors

Along those same lines...

"Condoms?" he asked, lips barely leaving mine.

"Mmhmm." I kissed him once more, then drew back and reached for the nightstand. As I was opening the drawer, Tristan's hand slid up my inner thigh, killing my concentration completely. How was he so good at that? One touch was like a magnet to a hard drive—totally blank. Not that I cared, though I did forget for a second why I was reaching into the drawer.

Condoms. Right. I found the strip, and—

Tristan pushed his thumb into my hole, and the condoms slipped out of my hand. Head falling forward, I whimpered with both pleasure and frustration.

"What's wrong?" he teased, pushing his thumb in again.

"N-nothing." I rocked back, seeking more that delicious penetration. "Goddammit..."

He laughed wickedly, and he said something I didn't catch because whatever he was doing with his thumb occupied all of my brain cells.

"Tristan..." I fumbled for the condoms that had slipped out of my hand. "Fuck..." I finally got hold of the strip and tossed it over my shoulder. "Would you just put one on and fuck me already?"

- Until the World Stops

Basically, condoms don't *have* to be a mood-killing "remember that sex can be risky" bucket of cold water on a scene. Just like anything in a sex scene, they can be used to enhance the tension, the heat, the emotional connection, or what have you. Be creative!

You can use them to keep the sexual tension amping up...

"Jesus Christ," he growled, pressing his erection against me as he dipped his head to kiss my neck. "I want... *Fuck*, I want you so bad."

Panting as his lips skated up and down the side

of my throat, I managed to whisper, "Do you have condoms?"

Dustin froze. He turned his head, furrowing his brow at the bedside table. "You know, I'm not sure if I do or not."

"Maybe we should check." I swept my tongue across my lower lip. "Before we need them."

"Good idea." He kissed me again, even as he pulled his body away from mine, like he knew we needed to pry ourselves apart but he just couldn't make himself go all the way.

"Dustin... check..."

Abruptly, he pulled away and started toward the bedside table, throwing a slurred, "Let me look" over his shoulder. I stayed up against the door because my knees shook too much to walk, and I was sure if I even moved, I'd wake up and this would be over.

Dustin pulled open the drawer. "I'll be damned." He reached in and pulled out the box. "I actually do."

"Oh, thank God." I started toward the bed, but then Dustin did a double take at the box in his hand, and the scowl that followed stopped me in my tracks. "What?"

He swore, dropped the box back in the drawer, and looked at me. "They're expired."

- All The King's Horses

Guess they're going to have to wait, aren't they? This results in them taking a late night trip to a store to pick some up, which ends up leading to an even hotter scene between two people who just can't wait a second longer.

Still keeping with the theme of expiration dates on condoms, Anna Zabo masterfully uses them in a scene with Max and Tom, who have been indulging in some seriously hot kink scenes in Max's home dungeon. Every time they've had sex, they've used condoms. Now they're in Max's bedroom for the first time:

Max levered himself up enough to wrench open the nightstand drawer and root around. He drew out a bottle of lube, then searched around in the drawer again. "Fuck. I don't usually—ah!" He drew out a condom. "Not expired. Thank god."

Max didn't regularly keep condoms in his bedroom. That flashed through Tom like lightning. He'd never considered that this—that he—wasn't normal for Max.

Cinnamon Roll
Anna Zabo

This prompts a line of conversation that builds on their dynamic and their relationship, but you'll have to read the book to find out how. (It's a great book, so I highly recommend it anyway!)

At the beginning of one of my ménage romances, Carmen is having a conversation with Isaac, who is married to her best friend, Donovan. They had a threesome recently to celebrate her long overdue divorce, and... well...

Finally, she spoke. "I'm pregnant."

The air in my lungs turned to lead, and the blood in my veins turned to ice. Had I been standing, my knees would have buckled as I stared at her, lips parted and eyes wide. When I could finally convince enough air to move to allow me to speak, I said, "Are you..." *Serious? Joking? Come on, Isaac, she wouldn't joke about that.* "...sure?"

She nodded slowly.

Holy. Fucking. Shit.

Carmen broke eye contact and exhaled. "I'm so sorry, Isaac, this is...it's..."

"Don't apologize." I stroked her hair. "We were just as much a part of this as you were."

"Well, one of you, anyway," she said dryly.

My hand stopped. Our eyes met again. The shock hadn't yet worn off, and up until she'd said that, I hadn't gotten that far yet.

Carmen wiped her eyes again and looked away. "Jesus, I can't believe I didn't even think to use condoms."

"No kidding." The words came out as little more than a hollow whisper.

Taut silence hung in the air. What was someone supposed to say? The marriage counselor in me probably knew what to say, but the man who'd just found out his best friend was carrying either his or his boyfriend's baby was, to say the least, at a loss for words.

And how the hell *did* we forget to use condoms? There was no doubt we were all pretty well trashed, especially if it even slipped Donovan's mind. He'd already become a father at an inopportune time once in his life; it wasn't something he took lightly. It wasn't something any of us took lightly.

I'd used protection in my single days, of course, but I'd been with Donovan so long it hadn't crossed my mind in years. And getting someone pregnant had just...it hadn't been something I'd ever had to consider when I was having sex. That night, it had just happened. Unplanned, unanticipated, without any second thoughts. And we were drunk and horny and...

Here we were.

- Who's Your Daddy?

Obviously this isn't a sex scene, and in fact the threesome in question doesn't happen on-page at all. The reason I included it here is to illustrate two things—one, some reasons why people might neglect to use condoms (alcohol, habit, heat of the moment, etc.), and two, how a condom (or lack thereof) can be a plot device. It also sets the stage for the sex scenes in the rest of the book: the three of them didn't use condoms before, and now Carmen is pregnant, so there's no need to use condoms going forward. They very briefly touch on this the first time they're in bed together, and that's the end of it.

In one last example, the characters in *World Enough and Time* use condoms at first. In fact, they don't have intercourse the first time they hook up because neither has any condoms, which then creates more tension for the next sex scene. Later in the story, though, Connor reveals to Dani that he had a vasectomy a few years ago, since he doesn't want to have children.

"Wait, that means that first night, when we didn't have condoms," I said, "we still could have had sex?"

He laughed. "Technically, yeah. But you'd only known me a few hours. Seemed like a bit much to ask you to trust me enough to go bareback, you know?"

"Fair enough."

He kissed me and whispered, "Though I have to admit, I would have loved to have felt you that way that night."

Wrapping my arms around him, I said, "It's not too much to ask now, is it?"

A grin played at the corner of his mouth. "I don't know. You tell me."

I kissed him. "Maybe we should get out of here."

- World Enough and Time

So condoms were a device to increase sexual tension early in the story, and later, the decision not to use them showed the deepening comfort and trust between the main characters.

The point of all of this is that condoms—and their expiration dates—can be great little plot devices that lead to all kinds of development. Again, be creative! Maybe one of your characters cheated on the other, and as they try to reconcile, the scorned partner wants to use condoms. A premature ejaculator might use them to help last longer. Along those same lines, a character who is so excited and turned on they're about to lose their minds might be glad they're using a condom so they don't come too soon. Or your characters might have reached a point where they trust each other enough to go without.

The possibilities are truly endless. This isn't real life where condoms mute sensation—condoms are only as boring or distracting as a writer makes them.

To Recap:

- The author should be aware of why a character uses or doesn't use condoms.
- Conversations about and use of condoms do not derail a sex scene—lazy writing does.

CHAPTER 12

PLEASURE FOR ONE
MASTURBATION

This is another sometimes hotly debated facet of erotic fiction. I've heard editors and authors alike state that masturbation scenes are invariably gratuitous. At best, they're purely for titillation without adding anything to the story. At worst, they relieve the sexual tension, which sort of defeats the purpose of building that tension to begin with.

Reader, I dissent.

The masturbation scene has endless potential. A character can get caught by someone else (the love interest, even). Or they can be listening in on someone else having sex (I show a snippet of this in the chapter on voyeurism). Maybe they're separated from their lover and need to relieve some tension, which just leaves them wanting more.

It can also be a means for a character to explore something they've never done before, as in this scene with Greg, who is only just coming to terms with his attraction to men. He's curious about anal penetration, but wants to try it himself before he tires it with another person.

I put the toy aside for a moment and opened one of the lube bottles. I poured some on my hand, leaned back against the pillows, and spread my legs.

The books recommended fingers first, so that was what I started with. The position was awkward —it'd probably be a hell of a lot easier with someone else doing the fingering. Or me fingering them. Except then I'd be a nervous wreck, so awkward positions would have to do for now.

Staring up at the ceiling with unfocused eyes, I pressed one finger in. Weird. Very...weird. I gritted my teeth, but that didn't help. And hadn't both Ethan and my reading material said that relaxing was important?

I closed my eyes and took a few slow, deep breaths. I concentrated on relaxing, and kept my fingertip there until the muscle finally obeyed. Pressing in this time, I had more luck—my finger slid in to the first joint. When I withdrew it and tried again, it still took some work, but the third time, it was easier. The burn was bizarre. This turned people on? Different strokes, maybe. Still, I was determined to give it a chance, and pushed my finger in again.

Little by little, I slid it deeper. After a while, I added a second, which didn't take nearly as much work as the first by itself. Before long, they were sliding easily in and out.

Okay. So fingers weren't bad. No pain. Weird, but no pain. In fact, the longer I did it, the better it felt. Still an intense burn, but not unpleasant. Kind of...kind of addictive, actually. Wow.

I blinked my eyes into focus and looked at the condom-covered toy beside me. I swallowed. Time to level up.

I slipped my fingers free, and had to pause for a moment to catch my breath. I wanted them back inside me. Like *now*.

Which meant I really, really wanted to get on with it with this toy, so I quickly put on some lube, not caring that a few drops landed on my stomach or ran down the side of my wrist. I'd probably take a shower after this anyway, so whatever.

- To Live Again

I would also argue that rather than relieving sexual tension, a masturbation scene can *amplify* sexual tension by showing how feverishly the character desires the love interest. I think some of this comes from the idea that having an orgasm relieves sexual tension, but that isn't really the case. It can relieve some of it temporarily, but the tension is going to come back tenfold before the character even catches their breath.

As far as how to actually write the scene, it really depends on what you're going for. The scene quoted above focuses a great deal on the physical actions and sensations. A scene in which someone is pining for someone else will likely concentrate more heavily on what the person is imagining, interspersed with mentions of what they're doing physically to get themself off.

As you approach such a scene, ask yourself:

- What is this character

imagining/hearing/seeing while they
masturbate?
- How do you want them to feel after the scene?
- How do you want the reader to feel during and
after the scene?

Remember, too, that if your answer is simply that you
want to turn your reader on and that you want your character to have a satisfying self-love session, that's totally fine!
As long as you know the purpose of your scene, you're good
to go.

To recap:

- Masturbation scenes are as valid as any other
sex scene.
- They can serve any number of purposes.
- Know going into it what you want the scene to
accomplish.

CHAPTER 13

SEX, DRUGS, AND—

YEAH, THAT'S PRETTY MUCH IT. SEX AND DRUGS.

Sooo...what if your characters do, shall we say, recreational substances? Should this affect your sex scene?

Most likely, yes.

First, remember that writing about your characters having sex under the influence doesn't mean you advocate doing so. I write about my characters murdering, stealing, and putting pineapple on their pizza. That doesn't mean I advocate any of those things. Well, except for the pineapple on pizza—that is correct and I will fight anyone who says otherwise.

Anyway. The point here is that you're writing your *character's* story. If your character would have sex under the influence, then there's nothing wrong with writing about it.

That being said, it is important to be cognizant of the implications of sex under the influence, even if those implications are just "they like having sex while stoned."

- Does the substance and dose affect their ability to give consent?

- Are they still in control of their mental and/or physical faculties?
- Would they engage in this activity if they were sober?
- Would they do so with this partner/these partners while sober?

If you're going to write your characters having sex under the influence of a substance, it's important to understand how that substance can and will affect their mind and body. For example, someone who is high on cocaine might have a spectacular time in bed, but be unable to orgasm. Substances like alcohol can lower inhibitions as well as the ability to consent. Erections can be difficult to achieve or maintain under certain substances, while someone can be downright priapic on others, just without the ability to orgasm. Sensation can be heightened. It can be numbed.

Lorenzo laughed, and I laughed, and I was dizzy and ridiculous and I didn't fucking care how stupid the joke had been. Still chuckling, he kissed me again, and it took a moment for both of us to stop laughing enough to really kiss. But then we did, and Lorenzo shifted onto one arm so he could stroke me, and I swear it was like a decade's worth of fear and stress had been booted out of the room in favor of all the liberating feelings that came with just letting go with someone. We had a foothold. We still had a lot of work to do, and there would still be plenty of risk and danger ahead, but for the first time in years, I felt like I might *win*.

Lorenzo broke the kiss again, shuddering as he fucked into my hand. "Oh, God..."

I bit my lip, gazing up at him and pumping him harder. It was sometimes tough for me to come thanks to the coke, but I'd been rationing it today, and it had been a couple of hours. The numbness in the back of my throat was gone. An orgasm was feeling not just possible, but inevitable.

- You Had One Job
Written with Cari Z

The specifics of each drug are not my area of expertise. I have written characters engaging in sex under the influence of marijuana, alcohol, cocaine, poppers (aka, amyl nitrate), and other drugs, but there are myriad ways each drug can affect each individual person. You'll want to research those things anyway if your character is using, and definitely explore the sexual side effects as well.

The reason I'm including this chapter, though, is to touch on what a writer should consider when writing sex while a character is under the influence.

Most importantly, *your character might not be entirely in control, but you must be.*

- How much has your character taken?
- Can your character give consent?
- How does you substance affect sensation, awareness, and performance?
- Has your character used the substance before? How is their tolerance?
- Is the substance illegal where they are? This can

cause heightened fear and danger if they're
concerned about getting caught, particularly if
the punishment is severe.

As always, do thy homework.

And keep in mind that some drugs have some, shall we
say, less than pleasant side effects that can put a damper on
sex. Cocaine and opioids have opposing effects on the lower
digestive tract that can make anal sex less than pleasant. Do
you need to include those? No. Just be aware that they *can*
be a thing.

To recap:

- Research your character's drug(s) of choice,
  including sexual effects.
- Be aware of how it affects their ability to
  consent and perform.
- Your character doesn't have to be in control, but
  you should be.

CHAPTER 14

TAKE A DEEP BREATH AND RELAX

ANAL SEX

First and foremost, this chapter is not just for writers of gay male romance. Anyone with an anus can engage in anal sex, and that includes characters in romance novels. A flesh-and-blood penis isn't even required thanks to dildos and strap-ons. If your straight guy is secure in his masculinity and his sexuality, he might even enjoy being pegged.

Also, anal sex scenes are not *mandatory* for gay male romance. Plenty of real live gay men never engage in it, or they don't always engage in it. Even if they're into it, it doesn't mean they're going to have it every time. Don't feel like your M/M characters *must* engage in anal sex.

Case in point:

Asher blushed. His fair skin always gave him away.

"Talk to me," I whispered. "Whatever it is."

"I..." His jaw worked. Then, all at once he met my eyes and blurted out, "Is anal a deal-breaker?"

It took a second for me to make sense of the question. "You don't want to?"

He blushed, biting his lip as he dropped his gaze, and slowly he shook his head. When he started talking, the words came fast and furious: "I can handle it, so if you really want it, then we can. It's not my favorite thing, but I—"

"Asher. Hey."

He looked at me, uncertainty etched all over his freckle-sprinkled face.

I caressed his cheek. "It's not a deal-breaker."

"It isn't?"

"No. Nothing is." His eyes were still full of skepticism, so I softly added, "When I said anything you want, that includes *not* doing anything you *don't* want."

The tension slowly melting out of his forehead and shoulders was heartbreaking. I knew all too well what it was like to feel strong-armed into things in the bedroom. How hard it was to try to put up boundaries when someone seemed bound and determined to test, break, and bulldoze every last one of them. And given everything he'd been through...

"I promise," I said, "nothing is a deal-breaker. I love anal, but if you're not enjoying it, then it's the last thing I want to do."

He searched my eyes, his expression still full of disbelief.

I smiled. "Did I give you any reason to believe I wasn't satisfied the first time?"

Asher shook his head. "But we couldn't fuck then. We didn't have condoms."

"And?" I shrugged. "I promise I didn't walk

away thinking, 'Damn, that would have been even better if I could have fucked him.'"

"Oh." He swallowed. "I just...don't want you getting bored."

I grinned, smoothing his hair. "We could stop at kissing, and I still wouldn't get bored."

The creases in his forehead screamed renewed skepticism.

So I leaned in and kissed him again, and I let that kiss linger for a long, languid moment. I slid my tongue alongside his, drawing a throaty moan out of him, and we didn't stop until we were both breathing hard. Looking in his eyes, I whispered, "You don't think that could entertain me for an entire night?"

- Rebound

This is from one of my two bestselling M/M romances *ever*.

Anal sex is *not* mandatory.

With that out of the way, let's talk about when we *do* write anal sex scenes.

As I've harped on plenty of times throughout this book, you don't want to accidentally make your characters or readers cringe or wince[1]. And with anal sex, there are plenty of opportunities to do just that:

- Not using lube.
- Not using enough lube.
- Not using something that actually works as lube.

- Not using lube that's safe to use with a condom.
- Not using lube.
- No prep, particularly with someone who's inexperienced or nervous.
- *Not using lube.*

See a pattern?

There are people who argue that anal sex can be done without lube as long as it's done carefully, but I'm pretty sure a lot of butts clenched up just reading that sentence. The prevailing wisdom is that you can never have too much lube. If your characters *are* going to go in dry, make it clear this is a deliberate choice and not an authorial oversight. Otherwise, lube is your friend. I mean, your characters don't need to have sex in a swimming pool full of AstroGlide or anything—though if you've written that scene, I kind of want to read it—but be generous with the stuff.

Then there's prepping. The anus is much tighter than a vagina, and going in too hard or too fast is a really good way to hurt someone. Going in vaginally without foreplay is one thing. Depending on the person and the situation, that *can* be pretty hot.

Anal generally requires a bit more care, and that's where prepping comes in. How much and what kind depends on the person. Rimming can relax the bottom, not to mention arouse them. Same with fingering, which can help stretch them in order to take a cock or toy. Not every person—and by extension not every character—needs thorough prepping before anal. An inexperienced bottom will most likely need more prep than someone with more experience, so your readers likely won't buy—or like—your virgin bottom being pounded by a nine-inch cock without so much as a cursory fingering.

And remember, this isn't just a boring, mechanical process—prep is part of foreplay! It's a great place to get your character (and reader) hot, not to mention show (and relieve) some tension.

Her hand drifted over his ass and between his cheeks. He reminded himself again to breathe, and forgot about that completely when a slick, warm-cool fingertip pressed against his anus. Alyssa didn't move it—she held it there, applying steady pressure, neither backing off nor pushing in.

"Breathe," she whispered. "Relax. I'll stop if it's uncomfortable."

Now that he was in this position, Shane couldn't begin to imagine how it could be comfortable, but he closed his eyes and exhaled slowly. Inhaled. Exhaled. Relaxed. Inhaled. Exhaled. Relaxed some more.

The pressure increased. He concentrated on not tensing up, and...

Oh God.

Her fingertip slid inside him. She withdrew it, pressed it in again. At least she didn't have long nails. That could've been...unpleasant.

She worked a second finger in, and the burn intensified. The friction was minimal—she didn't skimp on the lube at all—but the stretching sensation was oddly addictive. It felt...not good, but not bad either. Just incredibly intense. Completely alien. Weird, to say the least. He wanted more, and he wasn't sure he could take any more.

"I think you're ready." Her voice sounded a million miles away. "If it's too much, just say so."

He nodded. Didn't speak. Couldn't.

Her fingers slipped free. Though he knew it was coming, the thick, blunt presence against his ass was unnerving. And exciting. And terrifying. And...

Inside him.

He gasped.

Like she had with her finger, she withdrew, and then pushed in again, and his whole body trembled as if it were the first time he'd ever felt it. The third stroke, same thing—it was like the second the toy pulled free, his brain couldn't comprehend that those feelings had actually happened until they happened again and blew his mind all over again.

"This all right?"

"Yeah." He wasn't even sure where the word came from. It sounded like his own voice. But... whatever. He was too caught up in this bizarre feeling of being fucked and...and liking it.

"This isn't too much?"

Oh, it was definitely too much, but not in the way he expected.

"It's...good. Just like that." He paused, moistening his lips. "Faster?"

- I'll Show You Mine

Prepping is also a really good time to show the dynamics between your characters. Is your top conscientious and in-tune to the bottom? Is the bottom trusting and relaxed?

Does the top just force their way in? Does the bottom grit their teeth instead of saying anything? Maybe your top uses prepping as a way to tease the bottom, driving them wild until they're begging for the real thing. Maybe your experienced bottom doesn't entirely trust the top, or is feeling self-conscious for some reason, or is anxious about something else, and can't relax enough to go through with it.

At the end of the day, it's your call as an author how much prep and lube your characters need, and how that affects the sex as well as the characters and their relationship.

So Who's On Top?

There is no rule about who has to be on top. There's a cliched stereotype that if the characters are both men, the bigger/older/more dominant/more experienced/more masculine guy tops, but there's absolutely no reason your smaller/younger/subby/inexperienced/femme guy can't be on top. Anal sex does not have a *You Must Be At Least This Tall To Ride His Ass* sign.

Do be aware that in some times and cultures, there is an implied gender association with the top and bottom positions. Late 19th/early 20th century queer culture was emphatic about this, to the point that a man could be a top and still be considered straight. For more on this, I recommend reading *Gay New York: Gender, Urban Culture, and the Making of the Gay Male World, 1890-1940* by George Chauncey.

At least in contemporary times, though, this dynamic exists more as a stereotype than a cultural norm.

If your couple is straight, there's no reason the woman can't be on top. A Dominant can be a bottom and a submissive can be a top. Characters can switch. They can be exclusively a top or exclusively a bottom. The shy, passive person can be a top. The powerful CEO can be a bottom.

There are so many tropes, clichés, and stereotypes about who tops/bottoms and what it means to top/bottom, but the bottom line (so to speak) is it comes down to two things:

1. If they like how it feels when they take it up the ass.
2. If they like how it feels to give it up the ass.

That's it. And I don't just mean how they physically feel. Maybe bottoming feels too intimate or vulnerable. Maybe topping is too much pressure. Maybe they've just never gotten the hang of bottoming without discomfort. There might be some deep-seated baggage that makes them unable to even consider topping, or they might just not care for the physical sensation of bottoming.

Just don't fall into the trap of automatically and universally using a character's physical stature or financial status as the reason they top or bottom. I mean, it's one thing if those reasons make sense to your character. i.e., "I'm a billionaire with fifty thousand people working for me—I'm not taking it up the ass from *anyone*." But the bigger/richer/more dominant character doesn't *have* to be the top by default.

Now let's talk positions for a second. The assumption is usually that anal sex happens in a doggy style position. And there's certainly no reason to overlook that position. It's hot, it's primal, and it's probably the most versatile—it can be done over furniture, the back of a car, up against a wall, facing a mirror, etc. The bottom's clit or cock can be stimulated manually, either by their own hand or the top's.

So don't overlook rear entry, but it's hardly your only option. Anal can absolutely be done in the missionary position or with the bottom astride, for example. Really any position that can be accomplished with penis-in-vagina sex can work for anal. How much your characters can do depends on how limber they are and how much space they have, of course. If they're both six-foot-five, I might struggle to suspend my disbelief if they're trying reverse cowgirl in the backseat of a Geo Metro, but that would apply to anal or vaginal. If one's a gymnast and the other's a contortionist... well, let's see what that Geo Metro can handle.

Self-help sex books are your best bet here, especially those that focus on anal sex. They approach it from what's practical, doable, safe, and pleasurable, not what sounds hot on the page or looks good on camera. Then you can take it from there and make it hot with all the sensations, emotions, etc., we've talked about in the rest of this book.

If you're not sure if a position is doable, or how exactly it's doable, those guides are excellent resources. This is also where porn *can* come in handy. Beware, though, as mentioned in the chapter on porn—just because it's *doable* in a porno doesn't mean it's *comfortable*. Many of the positions used in pornos are meant for the pleasure of the camera, not the participants, and can actually be incredibly taxing or even painful. So particularly with the really acrobatic positions, porn is a dubious resource at best.

That said, especially with amateur porn, you can get an idea of where arms and legs wind up during this or that position. For example, you might notice in some gay porn that, in the missionary position, the bottom will protectively cup his testicles in his hand. Why? Because a pelvic bone slamming into a set of balls can really kill the mood. Does that mean you should always have your bottoming character cover their balls? No, but do be aware that in that position, those dangly bits are vulnerable to some, shall we say, unpleasantry. The character can cover them. The top can consciously position himself so the bottom's balls don't get squished. The bottom can get nervous and suggest a different position.

Be aware and mindful. I'm sure you're tired of hearing me say that, but I promise, it's that important!

So at the end of the day, anal sex scenes aren't all that different from penis-in-vagina scenes. There's more prep and artificial lube involved, but if you can write a penis-in-vagina scene, you can write an anal scene.

To recap:

- Anal sex is not mandatory in M/M, and it's absolutely doable with straight couples, F/F —anyone.
- Lube.
- Don't overlook prep.
- Lube.
- Tops and bottoms are what they are based on what they like, not *who* they are.
- *Lube.*

CHAPTER 15

PUTTING YOUR MONEY
WHERE YOUR MOUTH IS

ORAL SEX

I'm going to keep this chapter short, not because oral sex is unimportant, but because most of what I would say about it has already been addressed in previous chapters:

- Not everyone is into it.
- Orgasms make things hypersensitive for a bit.
- Focus on emotions and sensory details, not just the mechanical parts.
- Keep in mind what your characters were doing before the scene, and how that might affect smells and tastes.

What I will say is that oral is an often-overlooked opportunity for characters to be imperfect and give each other feedback. Everyone has their preferences and things that work for them; what an excellent chance for communication!

While the fantasy of a partner intuiting everything one needs is great and all, there is something unspeakably sexy about someone putting aside their ego, listening to what their partner is telling them, and applying that to give them pleasure. This is two-pronged: one person has to be confident and trusting enough to express what they want, and the other has to be able to take that as feedback and not an insult to their sexual prowess. Or, if you want the scene to go awry or the dynamic to get complicated, maybe that trust and confidence aren't there yet, or maybe the partner does take it personally.

The point here is that the person who intuits exactly what their partner wants without any feedback or direction is hot and all, but the alternative has so much potential for emotional engagement, bonding, and increasing or lessening tension. Neither is incorrect. Neither is better or worse. In some stories, the former is exactly what you need. But make sure you're not overlooking something that could add more tension or intimacy to your story.

Much like penetration, oral sex isn't mandatory in a book. Readers do enjoy it, and it's certainly sexy, but there isn't room for it in every story. You might have a character who's not into it, or your characters come from an era or culture where oral sex isn't done, or there simply might not be an opportunity to show it on-camera. Only you can decide what's appropriate for your characters and what fits your pacing and the story you want to tell; just don't feel like you have to shoehorn it in for the sake of meeting a particular quota of erotic scenes.

To spit, or to swallow?
That is the question

At least among hetero folks, there's a joke that "spit or swallow" is the difference between like and love. It's a joke, but to some, there's truth to it—if the person spits after their partner comes in their mouth, then it's less intimate, they don't love their partner, etc.

Personally, I think this is nonsense. Some people, regardless of their feelings for the other person, simply don't enjoy the taste or feeling of semen in their mouth. They'll fellate their partner to completion, but keeping it in their mouth or swallowing it is a hard limit.

It's up to you how your characters feel about this. The main reason I bring it up is to say that you don't have to make your characters swallow in order to show their love, and they don't have to spit if they're with someone casual. It all comes down to their personal preferences. Write what's true to your character, not what you feel pressured to write because of external expectations.

Now, what if your character feels that there's emotional significance to spitting or swallowing? What if they have strong feelings about their partner doing one or the other? That's okay! Characters are influenced by the world around them, same as we all are, and "controversies" like this exist for a reason. People really do have strong feelings about it. So it's perfectly reasonable for your character to be one of them.

Just make sure you're true to your character and your story, and you'll be fine.

Take it.
Yeah, all of it.

I'm kidding. Your character does *not* have to deep throat.

That's right. It's not required.

Some people just... can't. The gag reflex is a thing that exists, and especially if someone is new to giving head, it takes time and patience to train that reflex enough to deep throat. Even with that time and patience, sometimes it's not possible. Either the person panics because they feel like they're choking, or their jaw can't handle it, or any number of other reasons.

If your character cannot—physically or psychologically—handle deep-throating, they don't have to. Most of the sensitive areas of the penis are around the head anyway, so while deep-throating can be fun and all, it's not necessary to get a person off.

To recap:

- Oral sex is as optional as any other practice.
- Spitting or swallowing should be a personal preference, not a book requirement.
- Deep-throating is neither easy nor mandatory.

Part I
Sex on the Beach

If you own a TV or have ever been in the same room as one, odds are you've seen a particularly iconic moment from an old film called *From Here to Eternity*. In it, Burt Lancaster and Deborah Kerr roll around in the surf in a passionate embrace, doing as much of the nasty as the era's decency laws would allow.

There are two kinds of people in this world: people who think that scene is erotic and hot, and people who cringe, cross their legs, and wonder how much sand, saltwater, and sea life wound up in places it didn't belong. I can only assume that the people in the former category have never experienced what it's like to be in the crosshairs of the incoming tide. Remember, it isn't just water—the aforementioned sand and sea life is usually present and accounted for as well, and there are places that a person just should not have sand or sea life unceremoniously delivered via surf.

Clearly, we have reached the section where we're going

to talk about sex on the beach. And the thing is, sex on the beach is sexy as hell, but you know what isn't sexy? Sand. And you know what there is a lot of on beaches? *Sand*.

"But Lori," you're saying to your ereader or paperback or maybe even the audiobook, "it's a fantasy. My characters can totally have sex on the beach without getting sand everywhere."

Except... well...

Sand on a beach is like ants on a hill—as soon as you step on it, you're covered in it. The stuff sticks to you simply because you're located on a beach. Or just aware of a beach. I mean, really—all you have to do is look at a postcard of a beach, and suddenly there is sand in every nook and cranny of your car, clothes, shoes, and person. I lived on a tiny island for three years. I know of what I speak.

Okay, so maybe it's not that dramatic, but the point is, if you're rolling around in the sand, you're going to be covered in it, and chances are your character doesn't have a kink for "sex while pretending to be a sugar cookie." And the wetter the surface, the more sand sticks to it, *if you catch my drift*.

Yes, I'm being kind of silly here, but I'm serious too. Chances are, the last thing you want is for your reader to be cringing through your sex scene as they wonder just how much sand is being shoved into places it doesn't belong. (Spoiler Alert: A lot.)

So does that mean you should cancel that sex-on-the-beach scene? Does it mean you can't make it realistic and believable without making your reader squirm the wrong way? Of course not!

And in fact, it really doesn't take much. Have them put down a towel. Or even better—a blanket. Or have sex standing up. Or doggy style. Or put the bottom on top. Get creative!

I know it sounds like I'm killing the fantasy here, but the end result is really quite the opposite. Your reader will be able to get into the fun and heat of the scene without being yanked out of it by a jarring thought of "they are just *shoveling* sand into that character's—"

Because... ouch.

With a little foresight and creativity, you can write a perfectly sexy beach scene without all the grit.

"Do you have any idea how uncomfortable a hard-on is in a wet suit?"

"Oh, I think I have a pretty good idea." Shane's hands slid over my hips, and he pulled me back against him so I could feel how aroused he was. "Ever had sex on the beach?"

I licked my lips. "Ask me again in an hour, and I'll say yes."

"An hour?" His quiet laugh cooled my skin. "Oh, Eric, you'll be lucky if I get through the next few minutes without being inside you."

"Then it's a good thing we brought condoms, isn't it?"

"Yes, it is." He nipped my earlobe. "Why don't you get out of that suit, and I'll get a condom on?" He kissed the base of my neck and added, "Because I am so goddamned desperate to fuck you right now..."

Words. Lost on me. The best I could do was a nod, and he got the message.

We both got up and peeled off our wet suits, careful to keep sand off the towel and our hands. Whatever inhibitions I might have had were gone from the moment he'd kissed my neck, and I didn't know the meaning of nerves now. We were as out in the open and exposed as we could be, but there was no one else here. A broad expanse of water separated us from anyone who might give a damn about us, and with every touch, I lost my ability to give a damn about the consequences. I wanted him so bad I couldn't see straight now, and every move we made took us closer to the gratification of that first stroke.

My mouth watered as Shane stroked lube onto the condom. His hand stopped, and he took and held a deep breath like he needed a moment just to calm himself down. Then, slowly, he exhaled, and our eyes met. With a nod, he indicated the towel I'd been sitting on a moment before.

"On my knees?" I asked.

He nodded again. I thought he'd have some witty or dirty comment, but maybe he was as tongue-tied as I was just then.

I got on my hands and knees. When the sand shifted behind me, I closed my eyes, and Shane's hand materialized on my side.

- Conduct Unbecoming

See? Beach sex accomplished, all while keeping sand away from the critical areas.

As for scenes like the one in *From Here to Eternity*...

Look. If you want to write one like that, go for it. There's nothing wrong with writing something that's purely fantasy.

But some of your readers will inevitably remember the real-world aspects of the scene, and in reality, waves crashing over you like that is not all it's cracked up to be.

Let me tell you a story:

Many moons ago, I was out snorkeling a couple of miles off the coast of Okinawa. Thanks to a distant typhoon, the water was *really* rough that day. Not dangerously so, but enough that we had to swim harder than usual against the current. When we decided to call it a day, there was one problem: the tide was coming in, and we still had to get back on shore, which meant wading about twenty yards through shallow water while waves tried to knock us over.

After being rudely tripped by Poseidon a few too many times, I finally gave up and just let the waves wash me ashore.

Reader, when I tell you dead bodies have washed up with more grace than I did that day...

Anyway. The point here is that I can say with significant authority that lying on a beach and having a wave crash onto your person is not pleasant, and no amount of butt naked Burt Lancaster is going to change that. The sand, y'all. The *sand*. Not to mention the force of the wave. It wasn't even that big of a wave, but it was about as strong as the previous one that had deposited me on said beach, and that was, shall we say, *strong*.

Now imagine trying to get busy when one of those waves decides to slap sand.

Especially in more temperate places where *that water is cold*.

Do with that information what you will.

Part II

Cars & Showers

Similar principles apply to both beach sex and car sex. Sex in the backseat always makes for a steamy scene (remember the section on *Titanic*?). Ditto with getting it on in the shower. And fortunately, unless your characters have just been to the beach, there probably isn't any sand in the car or the shower.

Where cars and showers are similar to beaches is, quite simply, logistics. They sound hot and sexy, but in practice? Ouch.

Few things (like sand) can ruin a sex scene faster than the reader cringing and wondering when the character is going to slip and fall. Or realizing that 6'4" linebacker is going to be seriously stiff and sore after just getting into the backseat of that Geo Metro, never mind engaging in any thrusting. Or wondering how in the world they're engaging in all these acrobatics in the driver's seat when we all know the steering wheel is *right* there.

So am I telling you not to write sex on the beach or in a car or shower? Am I trying to ruin the fun and tell you everything should be realistic to a fault?

Absolutely not. Go forth and write thy fantasies.

It's just wise to understand and address the logistical concerns that might have your readers grimacing through your scene.

With those logistical concerns in mind, my general practice with scenes like these is to do one of two things:

- **Alleviate the issue**.
  - Put a towel down on the sand or have them figure out a position that minimizes sand in places where sand is unwelcome.

- Have sex over the trunk of the car instead of in the backseat.
- Consciously position themselves so they won't break their necks in the shower.
- Oral and manual. Save the intercourse for someplace more accommodating.
- **Tackle it head-on and make it part of the scene.**
- Give the characters a moment of silliness as they try to get comfortable in the back of a car.
- Let the character facing away from the shower get cold, and give the partner an opportunity to realize it, shift them around, and warm them up.
- Have them get frustrated with the situation and take it someplace else, which will just amp up the sexual tension.

Remember that sometimes awkwardness and clumsiness can add to a sex scene. The characters might laugh, which can be sexy in its own way because if the characters are comfortable enough with each other to laugh/be silly while they're having sex, that shows a certain degree of intimacy. Or they might be frustrated or nervous, which kills the mood, which can in turn give them something to bond over or cause tension between them.

Don't *ignore* the awkward bits—use them to your advantage!

The bottom line with scenes in tricky places is that you don't want the setting to steal the show. You don't want your reader thinking about sand in crevices, heads smacking into car doors, or how the character will explain to the paramedics how they broke their hip in the shower. The solutions to these issues may seem like they take all the fun out of everything, but they don't have to.

It's kind of like if you've ever been to a Cirque du Soleil performance. While the performers don't exactly cover their safety cables in Christmas lights or point them out to you, they're not invisible either. Sometimes they're out in the open, and sometimes you catch a glimpse when the light hits them just right. But the fact is, the cables are there and you really can't miss them. And you know what? It doesn't detract from the performance at all. In fact, I found a small amount of comfort in the occasional glimpse of a cable—I was there to see the acrobats perform, not die. A lot of people probably didn't even notice the cables at all, at least not until a performer fell and was able to land gently, get up, and try the stunt again without being any worse for the wear.

Think of my suggestions for these sex scenes as your semi-visible safety cables—you're not drawing attention to them, and the reader is, consciously or not, cruising along without worrying about uncomfortable logistics. It's like we discussed in the condom chapter—it doesn't have to be a big production. Just a subtle nod, and move on with the scene.

I acknowledge that it's entirely possible your readers won't think about this kind of thing at all. There are people who can watch the scene in *From Here to Eternity* without cringing and feeling phantom grit in intimate crevices. And that's perfectly fine. But it doesn't hurt to consider that many of your readers *will* think about it.

The way I look at it is this. If your readers won't be pulled out of the fantasy by concerns about sand or stiff necks, they also won't be pulled out of the fantasy by the author deftly making adjustments to avoid the same... and your readers who *would* notice the literal nitty gritty will be able to stay in the scene because you've kept your scene both believable and hot.

To recap:

- Cars are cramped and uncomfortable.
- Showers are slippery and dangerous.
- Sand is the glitter of the sea—it gets everywhere.
- Waves are strong, mean, and full of sand.

CHAPTER 17

THERE IS SEX AFTER 25...
BUT IT'S DIFFERENT.

If your dude is twenty-two and gets it up four times in a night, I'll probably buy it. If he's forty-five, my suspension of disbelief gets a little more tenuous. The fact is, the body ages, and that means changes in libido, stamina, and flexibility.

So does that mean we shouldn't write sex scenes involving anyone who isn't twenty-five and pristine? Of course not! It just means being aware of the limitations that particular character might face. My approach—don't shy away from their ages! If your characters are in their forties, acknowledge it head-on. Let them have joints that pop sometimes, or backs that don't tolerate acrobatic positions for quite as long. Let them *be* people in their forties, fifties, sixties, or whatever, and let them still be sexy and attractive in their own skin, not *despite* their age.

It sounds pretty obvious, I know, but I've read more scenes than I can count where the entirely normal human and not at all immortal/paranormal forty-something character has a priapic penis, the ability to go several rounds, and isn't the least bit sore the next day. And while it's kind of hot to imagine someone who can go and go and go, it's not realistic.

So does that mean it's not okay? You shouldn't write older characters who have the flexibility and stamina of characters half their age? No. Of course not.

But don't underestimate two things:

1. How quickly that might pull your readers – especially those of similar age to your characters – out of the story because it's unrealistic.
2. How real and sexy you can make your characters by *letting* them be forty-five.

Wait, what? How is it sexy to make a character's sex life reflect their age? Because it makes them more real. More human. More relatable. When your incredibly sexy forty-five-year-old's knee cracks or they need a little more time to recover, you're saying "feeling your age doesn't make you unsexy."

Maybe a character's neck hurts, or their hips aren't as flexible as they used to be. So, time to get creative with positions. Does their partner want to go another round, and though the mind is willing, the body hasn't *quite* recovered yet? That's why the good lord gave you a mouth, dudebro. Get down there.

Okay, I'm kidding about that last part. Kind of. Sometimes people are just done for the night, and that's fine. And as people get older, it gets more common.

Cuddle. Kiss. Talk about what they're going to do when they're both back in the game. Get creative.

This can also make things interesting when you have a May-September[1] relationship. When one character is young and spry, and the other is feeling the effects of a few more years, it's bound to come into play in the bedroom. Is Mr. September going to try to grit his teeth through positions that aren't as comfortable anymore because he's afraid of Mr. May getting bored? Will Mr. May subsequently feel guilty when Mr. September can barely move afterward, and handle him with kid gloves going forward?

Do you have to write your characters showing the toll Father Time takes on their bodies and their libido? Of course not. Fantasy and all that.

But remember that many of your readers—particularly those reading your stories with older characters—are likely older themselves. Readers love to see themselves on the page. You will earn the undying loyalty of those readers if you can not only engross and arouse them, you can make *them* feel sexy in their own no-longer-twenty bodies.

The bottom line is that sex after forty can absolutely be sexy, but it is *different* from sex in the twenties. By putting those differences on the page, you'll make your characters— and their sex scenes—even more real and believable.

Somewhere in all the kissing and groping, we wound up on our sides again. I wrapped my fingers around his cock, shivering at the groan that escaped his lips. Then he did the same, and his first stroke made me gasp. He kissed me again, and we stroked each other as we kept right on exploring each other's mouths. The feedback loop was amazing— the more hungrily we kissed, the more frantically we pumped each other, and the more frantically we pumped each other, the more hungrily we kissed.

In a moment of delirious arousal, I thanked God I couldn't get off as quickly as I had in my younger days, because even forty-five-year-old me would have come all over Terry by now. Like this, we could keep going, sending each other higher and savoring every moment of hot, mind-blowing bliss.

- The Walls Between Hearts

In the same book...

A thrill shot through me. Deep down I'd always regretted missing out on being a young gay man—indulging in things like making out in a theater or sneaking off to fool around—but something about this felt like a taste of the things I hadn't known I'd wanted back then. Except we *weren't* a couple of teenagers or twenty-somethings. We were grown men with sure kisses and confident hands. All the desire of young lovers with all the experience that came from all the partners we'd had over long decades, with no reason to rush and no one to hide from, and I decided then and there that this was well worth the sixty-one years it had taken me to get here.

We stroked each other slowly in between breathless kisses. Just touching and tasting and teasing. Enjoying each other with no rush to get naked or get off.

I don't care if I ever come as long as you don't go.

- The Walls Between Hearts

Don't let the young folks have all the fun!
To recap:

- Sex doesn't have to get less sexy with age.
- Your older readers will appreciate your older characters living it up and being sexy.

CHAPTER 18

WHIPS AND CHAINS AND FLOGGERS, OH MY!

A BDSM PRIMER.

In recent years, for better or worse, there's been a rise in BDSM in erotic romance. Some writers clearly know what they're talking about. Some... do not. And this is where a sex scene—indeed, an entire book—can get into abusive and even dangerous territory. Sometimes it's deliberate—dark romance is a thing, and that's fine.

But sometimes it's done inadvertently, especially if a writer doesn't completely understand kink.

I am not going to give you a comprehensive education on BDSM here. I have neither the space nor the expertise. What I will do, though, is offer a general primer and point you in the direction of those who can give you the more in-depth knowledge that will help you write realistic BDSM.

One thing to keep in mind right off the bat is that a BDSM scene isn't necessarily a sex scene because BDSM doesn't necessarily include sex. For some people, sex and BDSM are indivisible. For others, they can easily have one without the other.

In fact, sometimes a scene involving kink can be completely devoid of a sexual or even erotic component. In this scene from *The Master Will Appear*, Ryan is in another state, talking to Misha on the phone after a particularly emotional day with his semi-estranged mother. (When Misha is in the role of Dom, Ryan calls him Mikhail; the rest of the time, he's Misha)

"Are you alone?" Misha asked.

"Yeah."

"In your bedroom?"

"My mom's guest room." I didn't know why I corrected him. Why it mattered. Maybe because this didn't feel like anything that was *mine*.

"Ryan."

I managed, "Yeah?"

"Get on your knees." Still not a command. Still Misha. A harder edge, but still...not.

Closing my eyes, I released a heavy breath. "Misha, I'm not in the mood to—"

"Just trust me." His voice was so gentle, it almost shattered the last of my composure. Then, a little harder, he said, "Get on your knees, Ryan. Now."

My whole body suddenly felt so heavy, all I'd have to do was let gravity do the work. Slowly, I did as I was told, and eased myself down onto the thick gray carpet. "Okay. I'm on my knees."

"Good." That single syllable of approval made fresh tears prick at my eyes, and at the same time, let a little ray of light break through the dark cloud that had been over my head since I'd landed in New York.

I exhaled, but said nothing.

"I want you to imagine I'm there, Ryan." A weird combination of Misha and Mikhail. "Sitting on the edge of the bed. With you kneeling there at my feet. Can you picture it?"

I nodded but then remembered he *wasn't* here and almost choked on my voice as I whispered, "Yeah. I can."

"Would you like it if I let you lean against me? Stroked your hair?"

There was no stopping the tears now, but I at least tried to keep them out of my voice. "Yeah. I would. A lot."

"When you get home, I will. For now, this is the best I can do. I'm not there with you, but I'm here. As long as you need me to be." He paused, and his voice was like a warm caress, "I want you to lean on me, Ryan."

And just like that, I broke.

- The Master Will Appear

So as you can see, sex and eroticism are not mandatory in scenes involving kink. I would argue that the one and only thing that is *absolutely paramount* in BDSM is consent. I've already discussed the issue of consent at length in a previous chapter, so I won't repeat all that here, but it's a common thread in nearly all literature about real-life BDSM. The mantra "safe, sane, and consensual" isn't just a catchy slogan—it's a core tenet of BDSM. Much like the submissive is trusting their Dom to provide them with a safe, sane, and consensual scene, your reader is trusting you to do the same.

That's not to say a kinky scene can't or shouldn't go wrong. Things happen. Not every Dom or sub knows what they're doing, and even if they do, they are (presumably) human. No one knows how to swing a flogger perfectly the first time they pick it up. No one masters Shibari the first time they pick up a rope.

Basically, a character can be a complete and utter BDSM disaster, but the author needs to know *exactly* what they're talking about. To echo the drumbeat you've encountered numerous times in this book, problems in BDSM should be written deliberately and for effect, not occur because of the author's ignorance or apathy.

It's like writing in general—you need to learn and understand the rules in part so that you can effectively bend and break them. If you understand how flogging works, then you'll know where the Dom might start feeling fatigue, and where on the sub they'll want to avoid hitting in order to prevent injury. You'll know what will happen if the swing of the flogger isn't precise, and how the tails might wrap around and *really* hurt. In a sense, understanding every detail gives you the freedom to write characters who don't, and with believable consequences.

You don't have to write perfect BDSM any more than you need to write perfect anything else. Flaws are what make us human, and those flaws can come out in the dungeon. The key is *knowing* when you're writing something imperfect. It means not presenting us with a disaster and telling us it's ideal.

Unfortunately, this is a thing that happens all too often in erotic fiction. I have read far too many scenes that were—objectively—sexual assault masquerading as BDSM. I've read scenes where Doms have ignored safewords, abandoned bound submissives, or took advantage of an immobile sub and crossed previously agreed-upon boundaries. I've even read multiple stories in which a Dom let others have sex with the submissive while that submissive was too far into subspace to know what was happening, never mind consent.

These scenes are not intended to be horrific or criminal —they're intended to be hot. The Dom is not written as a villain, but as a hero. The reader is expected to be fanning themselves, not trying to keep their lunch from coming up.

Of course you can absolutely write dark and twisted BDSM. But call it what it is. If you're not writing dark fiction, and your aim is for safe, sane, consensual kink, it's still totally fine to have your characters mess up. Just make their actions have consequences. If your Dom ignores a safe-word, that's a major breach of trust. Can you write a Dom who ignores a safeword? Of course. As a reader, I'll want to know why, and I'll want to know how the submissive feels about it. I'll want to know how the Dom is going to win back the damaged trust. If the submissive's trust in the Dom *isn't* damaged, my trust in you as the author will be.

Basically, there is no law that says your Dom can't ignore a safeword, but I as the reader will be looking askance at them for it until they acknowledge it, apologize for it, and redeem themselves for it. And if they don't, and the story continues with that character as the flawless romantic hero, I'll be looking askance at *you*.

Speaking of safe words, it is also okay for characters to use safe words without it being a disaster. It can be as simple as a character realizing they're not in the mood, or even someone getting a muscle cramp or losing a contact lens. Which, as with many things, can be an opportunity for characters to show and demonstrate trust and concern for each other.

Safe words aren't just for subs, either. Everyone involved in a scene can (and arguably should, depending on who you're asking) have one. Don't underestimate the myriad ways you can bring a safe word into your kink.

In Anna Zabo's *Cinnamon Roll*, Tom—a sub who's been mistreated by Doms in the past who didn't respect safe words—is doing a demo with Max, who is hoping to (later on) show Tom what a good Dom is like:

Tom crossed his arms and considered this. His acting was decent. "We didn't talk safewords."

"I was thinking traffic lights."

"Ah, red, yellow, green." Tom nodded. "Those are easy to remember. We can use those."

The ease at which they fell into the teaching together was remarkable. Together, they moved through negotiating consent and safewords, what to do when using a gag, and touched briefly on types of situations where partners might not use safewords, but rely on other ways of communicating.

"There's a lot of trust involved," Max finished. "So be sure you have a partner who respects you."

"Sir?"

Tom addressing him as such flared deep pleasure in Max. "Yes, Tom?"

There were spots of color on Tom's cheeks. "Do you have a safeword?"

"Yes, yes I do. It's *flower*." He focused solely on Tom for a moment. "Thank you for asking."

The hesitant smile Tom gave Max was *everything*. He savored it like a small sip of fine wine, then turned to their audience. "That's something I should mention: both Dom and sub absolutely have the ability—and should—end a scene if they don't feel comfortable."

"Consent," Tom said, "works both ways." He voiced that as if this was the first time he'd considered the concept.

Max shoved down the anger in his chest. "Yes, it does."

- Cinnamon Roll
Anna Zabo

And even when a character knows they can use a safe word, they might still feel bad about it. Like they failed their Dom (or sub), for example.

Here, Aaron uses a safe word because he got too far up in his own head and panicked. Will and Kelly immediately untie him, of course, but Aaron still has feelings about it.

Will slowed, and I was pretty sure it was his hand that came to rest on my hip. "Aaron." His soothing Dom voice made my burning skin tingle. "Are you all right?"

Moistening my lips, I nodded. "Yeah."

Why does that feel like a lie?

"I'm good," I insisted, not sure if I was telling Will or myself.

"Aaron." He stroked a hand over my hip. "Talk to me."

"I can..." I could handle this. Of *course* I could

handle this. I wanted this. I'd been craving it. Twisting in the wind without it. Climbing the walls while we'd tried to find someone who could give it. Now I had it. What was wrong with me?

Why can't I get into this the way I should?

But even through the haze of pain and sex and the barrage of unwelcome emotions, I knew that I couldn't get into it, and that if I tried to push through, I'd regret it. So would Will and Kelly.

I squeezed my eyes shut and fought back the shame and embarrassment that tried to keep my voice in my throat, and I finally managed: "Yellow."

Instantly, Will stopped. No more wax landed on my back. The smell changed to the distinctive acrid, smoky scent of a candle that had been extinguished. My heart sank. We were really done, weren't we? We needed to be, but it was disappointing.

A gentle hand rested on my hip. "You all right?"

I nodded. "Y-yeah. Yeah, I think I just..." I shivered, and not in a good way. "I can't do it."

Will pulled out. Sighing, I let my forehead rest on the flogger horse. I'd occasionally used a safe word if I had a hip cramp or we'd been going so long I needed to pause for some water, but it had been a long, long time since I'd had to use one because I just couldn't handle what we were doing.

Tonight, though...

Tonight I had.

And I felt like shit.

- Extra Whip

Of course, Will and Kelly reassure and soothe him. Everyone has complex feelings about it, but they communicate, and soon, they're on the same page again... especially Kelly—who's new to playing with Aaron and Will, and is sure he screwed up and is going to be jettisoned.

Even as the three of us shifted our attention to the TV and tried to settle on a movie, my mind stayed on that brief conversation, and the relief hung in there too. Earlier this evening, I'd been so sure this thing between us had imploded and there was no going back, but more and more, I believed them when they said a safe word wasn't the end of the world. Tonight hadn't been a good night for Aaron, so we'd shifted to Plan B: dinner and a movie. And slowly, I was relaxing into it as much as they clearly had.

When tonight's disaster had turned out to be nothing more than a minor hiccup instead of a major setback or a dealbreaker, it had made me realize just how much I'd thought I was about to lose. Because the thing was, I wasn't just worried about losing access to the kinky play. Aaron and Will were the only people I knew in town. I was still getting to know them, but they were basically my only friends in Laurelsburg.

I don't want to lose this.

I don't want to lose the two of you.

I *hadn't* lost this, and I *hadn't* lost them, and after seeing with my own eyes how little drama there was when a safe word came into play, I was way more secure about playing with them than I'd been from the start. Seeing was believing, and going forward, I could absolutely believe that they weren't just blowing smoke when they said a safe word wasn't a dealbreaker.

This thing we were doing promised to be absolutely amazing.

And after tonight, it felt even safer than before.

- Extra Whip

These are just some of many ways a safe word can be used for more than just slamming the brakes on a scene gone wrong.

Write the BDSM that suits your story, but when it takes a dark turn, call it what it its.

As I mentioned in the chapter on consent…

Adding leather to a rape scene doesn't make it BDSM. It makes it a rape scene with leather.

I know, I've harped on this a lot. But it's a common problem, and one that I think deserves attention.

Moving on from that, let's talk about when it *is* safe, sane, and consensual.

Where do you even start?

Well, presumably if you're writing kink, you've decided your character has a predilection for some kind of kink. Maybe they want to explore something new. Maybe they have years of experience. Questions to ask yourself…

- What is this character's kink?
- How much, if any, experience do they have?
- How much, if any, experience does their partner have?

- Do they have any fears, concerns, or traumas associated with this kink?
- Does their *partner* have any fears, concerns, or traumas associated with this kink?
- What are their safe words, and how does everyone involved feel about their use?

From there, decide how you want to show this kink in your story, and how significant it is to the progression of the story, to the dynamic between the characters, and to your character's development. An exploration could dominate (pardon the pun) your story, or it could be something that happens in the background. Your characters might dabble a little and decide it's not their thing. Whatever fits your characters and your story.

So when you get to individual scenes, how much do you describe? Do we need a play by play description of every knot in the intricate bondage? Only if that serves your story. In general, remember to focus on sensations, emotions, and interactions more than the mechanical parts. Your reader isn't going to be invested in how many times the Dom hits the sub with the flogger. They're going to be invested in how much the sub struggles to obey the Dom by counting the strokes out loud. They're going to be invested in how pleased and aroused the Dom is by the sub trying so hard to please them.

Don't tell us your sub is intimidated by the Dom. Show us sweat rolling down skin. Show us goose bumps and wide eyes. Show us trembling hands. Let us feel the pounding heart and the profound relief every time the Dom offers praise.

In terms of characters' actual kinks and practices, those will vary, as will how much you actually show on-screen and how intense it is. For example, kink doesn't *have* to be hardcore. I've referenced my *Extra Whip* and Anna Zabo's *Cinnamon Roll* a number of times in this book, and they offer a comparison in terms of how hardcore pain play can get. While sadomasochism is a significant part of the dynamic in *Extra Whip*, the focus is more on the developing trust and a relationship with Kelly, the third brought in by Aaron and Will to give Aaron the pain that is beyond Will's limits. As such, it's fairly late in the book before the pain starts getting into more hardcore territory, and even then, it's still relatively tame, simply because the foundation of trust is still developing.

By contrast, the characters in *Cinnamon Roll* jump right into hardcore sadomasochistic play, and their relationship grows from there. Early on, Tom and Max engage in far more substantial pain play than Will, Aaron, and Kelly do during their story. Both books had as much kink and pain as their stories needed and as their dynamics allowed. Had Will, Aaron, and Kelly gone as hard as Tom and Max, especially early on, it would have been a disaster for their relationship. Had Tom and Max gone as light as the triad, one or both of them would've likely been bored and lost interest before the romance had a chance to take hold.

Let your characters, their dynamic, and your story determine how much play needs to occur, and how much of it needs to be shown. Don't feel like you must include this or that kink element, even if your characters enjoy it. Focus on what your characters *and* their story need. If your characters are into bondage, but there's no place for bondage within the story, then don't sacrifice your pacing or derail your story just to shoehorn in a bondage scene.

Similarly, if your characters have fairly specific kinks—say, if your submissive enjoys being cuffed and flogged—

don't feel like you *must* add kinky variety for its own sake. Vary your scenes, of course, the same way you would your vanilla scenes. Make each scene unique and interesting, and make sure it develops your characters and moves your story. But don't feel like you need to add variety in the form of different kinks if they don't fit.

As you write your kink scenes, don't underestimate the depth and versatility of aftercare scenes.

Yes, Tom was crashing from the scene, but this was more than that, and it made Max want to hunt down every last one of Tom's exes.

Tom looked up and focused on Max. "You want to sleep in the same bed with me?"

Max nodded. "If that's okay with you."

Tom furrowed his brow. "Yeah, it's fine. I just— don't understand why."

Oh my god, Tom. Max bit his tongue to keep that exclamation in, then he spoke. "Can I explain tomorrow? I don't think either of us is up for the conversation tonight."

Tom seemed to accept this. "Yeah. Yeah, you're right."

So finally—finally—he got Tom into bed. Once there, Tom melted into the mattress, enough so that he barely grumbled when Max tended to his well-abused ass. "Don't need anything."

"Humor me," Max said. "I like giving aftercare." He wondered if Tom even understood the concept.

"Oh," was all Tom managed, before mumbling something unintelligible and dropping into sleep.

- Cinnamon Roll
Anna Zabo

This is also an example of how the aftercare scene can contrast dramatically from the BDSM scene before it and still complement it. It shows us the soft, tender side of the sadistic Dom as he gently eases his submissive back into the real world. This is such an excellent opportunity for intimacy and affection.

It's also an opportunity for more sexiness:

Ryan could barely walk, and keeping an arm around him was tricky when I wanted to avoid making those welts burn even more. He was coming out of subspace now, the endorphins tapering off, and that kind of pain wouldn't be enjoyable for either of us.

"Careful." I guided him toward the bed. "Watch your step."

With help, he shuffled across the room, and I eased him down onto the mattress on his stomach. Sluggishly, he folded his arms under his head and closed his eyes.

"Don't move," I said. "This might sting a little."

He nodded but didn't open his eyes. He'd been through this enough times now he knew what to expect, but it was easy to forget those details in that floaty space he was in. Startling him with the burn of lotion would turn this experience unpleasant.

I carefully smoothed lotion onto his tender skin,

pausing whenever he jumped. The welts were still an angry red. Tomorrow, they'd be pink, probably even purple in some places. Some subs bruised more easily than others, and Ryan was one who usually had satisfyingly dark bruises. Not deep ones. Not signs I'd actually injured him. But evidence that I'd been there. That I'd marked him.

Electricity crackled along my spine as I gently trailed my fingers across those marks, and I grinned to myself. I loved seeing and feeling my handiwork on his body. Knowing he'd still feel me tomorrow. Knowing he'd be able to see what we'd done for days. I suppressed a shiver and continued smoothing on the lotion.

- The Master Will Appear

You can also show us what happens when a Dom neglects to take care of their sub, and skipping aftercare doesn't have to be out of malice. Your character could simply be inexperienced. Or maybe they don't realize how much aftercare their specific submissive needs. It's an opportunity for your character to make a mistake and either make the situation worse or atone for it.

Whether it's a kink scene, a vanilla sex scene, or an aftercare scene, everything you show or don't show tells the reader something about your characters and their relationship. Make sure we're getting the message you want us to get.

So what about getting the technical details right?

As with everything else... research.

If you've never used a single tail, do some reading. Find

out what it actually feels and sounds like. Where will it actually hit? Where *shouldn't* it hit?

For this, I recommend reading articles written by and for Dominants/sadists for real-life play. It's generally advised to avoid striking places including but not limited to the kidneys and the spine, but this is an area best left to those with more expertise than I can claim.

If you're writing bondage, same thing, especially since there are different types of bondage—suspension bondage, predicament bondage, Shibari, etc. Make sure you know which type(s) your character enjoys and understands. Read up on knotwork and types of rope.

Is your Dom safety conscious? Do they keep paramedic sheers nearby? Do they constantly check feet and fingers to make sure there's no coolness or loss of sensation? Do they check in with the sub regularly for the same? Are they mindful never to leave a bound submissive alone? These are important things that a conscientious Dom would consider. One who's less experienced or is going to make some mistakes might have issues here.

There are plenty of books out there that are a wealth of information about BDSM and the various practices that fall under that acronym. You will find some listed after the last chapter of this book.

As you can see, there's a ton to look into. And don't be intimidated or discouraged by the research—you'd be amazed how much inspiration you can find as you're learning about a particular kink. By the time you have a full understanding of what you plan to write, your characters may be engaging in scenes or kinks you hadn't even imagined before. Keep an open mind!

To recap:

- Safe, sane, and consensual… unless you make a conscious decision to deviate from this for the purpose of your story.
- There's a lot to research—but you can find tons of inspiration!
- Not all BDSM has to be hardcore.
- Every character and relationship is different, and so are their kinks.
- Don't forget the aftercare.

CHAPTER 19

DELIVERED IN DISCREET PACKAGING

TOYS IN SEX SCENES

Let's talk toys! And also trips to go buy toys!

What is a toy, exactly? Well, it's any implement brought in to enhance the sexual experience. They can be small, like nipple clamps, handcuffs, or dildos. It could probably be argued that some of the larger pieces of BDSM furniture count as toys—the St. Andrew's Cross, for example, which is an X-shaped device to which a person's wrists and ankles are tied so they can be flogged, whipped, or otherwise tormented at their Dom's pleasure.

Toys are very common in—but are certainly not limited to—BDSM scenes. A frequent misconception is that kink always = pain, but this isn't the case at all. Many toys are used to cause other stimulation, such as heat/cold, tickling, electrical stimulation, etc. Some are penetrative, like butt plugs, dildos, and prostate stimulators.

Ice can be used (with care to prevent frostbite) to cause intense cold. Someone can put a cough drop or a peppermint in their mouth before engaging in oral sex to create a cold sensation as well, though if you don't want your reader to slam your book shut and run away screaming "ACK!

Yeast infection!", make sure your character isn't putting something sugary in their mouth before cunnilingus.

And sometimes multiple toys can be used together to intensify the effect, such as using handcuffs to restrain someone before engaging in tickle torture with a feather or a cat toy.

Sometimes certain toys won't work with a particular character. In this scene, Kent is teaching Carlene how to use a Wartenberg wheel (which is a spiny wheel at the end of a handle about the length of a pen or pencil). Ideally, Kent would have James bound and blindfolded, but James has some PTSD that would be triggered by either of those things. So, as an alternative, Kent simply orders James to remain still and keep his eyes closed. This results in James being able to engage fully in the scene without his psychological minefields being tripped, and it has the added bonus of forcing him to work harder to obey, which Kent and Carlene—both Dominants—greatly enjoy.

Carlene turned to Kent again, eyebrows up as if to ask if it was okay to proceed. He nodded.

She picked up the Wartenberg wheel and played with the pinwheel, pressing it with her fingers, spinning it, rolling it across her own skin. The sound was subtle—little metallic creaks and squeaks—but James's muscles twitched and tensed. With his eyes closed, his other senses would be extra alert, so he probably heard every tiny sound while his imagination thought of a million different things that might happen once those spikes touched him. And a million different *places* where they might touch him.

Kent grinned. Carlene was obviously getting a feel for the implement before she put it on her husband's skin, but she'd noticed his discomfort, and she started capitalizing on it. Spinning the wheel harder so it would squeak louder. Leaning closer to him and rolling it across her own arm.

Kent cleared his throat. She turned, and he made a gesture like he was running his fingers across his arm, then pointed at James. The wicked grin that spread across her lips went straight to Kent's balls—confident or not, she was definitely getting into this.

Carlene spun the wheel enough to make a high buzzing sound, and before that had even begun to slow, she reached for James with her free hand and let her fingertips brush just beneath his navel.

James damn near came up off the bed, and Kent damn near came unglued. Carlene did it again, trailing her fingertips along James's hipbone, and her husband gripped the sheets, his knuckles whitening and every muscle in his torso contracting beneath her soft touch.

Then she brought the Wartenberg wheel closer to his chest. Just before she touched the spines to his skin, though, she hesitated.

Kent's heart skipped. *Come on, Carlene. Come on, you've got this.*

He opened his mouth to encourage her out loud, but then she flipped the Wartenberg wheel around in her hand, holding it like a pen, and drew its metal end—its undoubtedly *cold* metal end— around James's nipple.

James sucked in a breath, and his back arched.

His teeth snapped shut, and Kent chuckled. *Almost let something slip out, did you?* But he was getting the hang of it. Though his senses were probably all kinds of overwhelmed right then, he remembered that he wasn't allowed to speak.

Carlene drew little circles and swirls all over his chest and stomach. The metal was probably starting to get warmer now, and he didn't jump quite like he had on first contact.

Not until she flipped the wheel over again.

And rolled the spikes just above his hipbone.

James gasped so hard, he clapped his hand over his mouth like he'd *just* stopped himself from letting go of more than a stifled, strangled moan. His eyes flew open for a split second, but he quickly squeezed them shut.

- Kneel, Mr. President

Some toys won't work for some characters, like James, but for others, toys can be a very effective and sexy way for people to compromise when one person's desires collide with their partner's limits. In this scene, Alec is absolutely not interested in giving or receiving anal sex, but Bryce very much enjoys penetration.

Alec pulled a black plastic tote down from the shelf above his hanging clothes. It wasn't huge—maybe like the size of a shopping basket—and something rattled as he brought it over to his bed.

When he pulled off the lid, I peered inside, and

I couldn't help but whistle. "Oh, wow. You *do* have a few, don't you?"

"Well, I never know what size someone might like or if they want something that vibrates." Alec shrugged, gesturing at everything from finger-slim vibrators to get-that-thing-away-from-me-thick dildos. "It's only good manners to at least try to accommodate guests as best I can." He paused. "And I promise they're all thoroughly cleaned, plus I always put condoms on them."

I nodded. "Yeah, I figured." I'd shared toys with people before, and though I hadn't known Alec very long, I wasn't at all surprised that he was careful about cleanliness and hygiene.

"So." He glanced at me and bit his lip, looking unusually self-conscious. "Do any of them appeal? Or if there isn't something that works for you or you're not comfortable with something that's been used, I'd be more than happy to order something for—"

"Nah, no need for that." I studied the options a little closer. "I've used toys with guys before. Long as they're clean with a condom over it, it's all good."

He nodded, still seeming slightly uneasy.

I looked into the box again and quickly found one that would work. "How about this?" I pulled it out and admittedly felt kind of ridiculous, holding up a thick dildo like it was the prize I'd chosen after winning tickets at Dave & Buster's. "Do I have enough tickets for this one?"

Alec laughed, rolling his eyes. "No, I'm afraid you'll have to win a few more to pick that one."

- Bryce, Gentlemen of the Emerald City, book 3

By incorporating toys, they can spice up their encounters, and they can also make sure Bryce is getting something he enjoys while Alec doesn't have to compromise a hard limit. Plus, now there's an opportunity for a fun and sexy scene where they explore something new together.

Even going shopping for a sex toy can be fun and explorative, not to mention give the characters a chance to bond, get to know each other, or just have a laugh together.

I gave Alex a moment to look around.

For me, this place was as natural and benign an environment as a grocery store. Totally comfortable, totally normal, and I was probably as familiar with the merchandise and its placement as the staff. Quite possibly more so. Put me in this or any sex shop in Seattle and I was like a bloodhound. I could find anything in minutes. Ethan had even tested the theory, coming in here with a stopwatch and a list of twelve items. Nipple clamps, a porn DVD featuring a particular actor, watermelon-flavored condoms, a bunch of other crap. I found everything in seven minutes flat.

Alex, however, was another story. His eyes were as big as the cock rings on the display beside him. He slowly scanned the store—all the way to the left, all the way to the right, back again—and gulped as he took in his surroundings. I followed the same trajectory, trying to imagine how it all appeared to someone as uncorrupted as Alex. By the time I'd set foot in a place like this for the first time, I'd had

several lovers and watched plenty of porn. Alex...
hadn't.

It didn't help that the sales staff either got really bored at times or were just insanely creative about displaying merchandise. Blowup dolls were arranged along the tops of shelves or suspended from the ceiling, most in hilariously compromising positions. One male doll had toys crammed into every available orifice, plus cock rings around his limbs, probably to emphasize the appearance of muscles. On his head, someone had fastened a bright pink strap-on. Not far from him, an O-mouthed female doll with a set of plastic Yoda ears on her head stood opposite another doll wearing a Darth Vader mask, and they were frozen in a duel with a pair of three-foot dildos.

All around the store were numerous flyers announcing specials, sales, visits from porn stars, things like that. I wondered if Alex noticed the papers were all held in place by stainless steel nipple clamps.

I couldn't be sure, but I thought he muttered something about not being in Kansas anymore.

- The Closer You Get

When you're bringing toys into a sex scene, get creative! There are plenty of ways to put toys to use, even those that seem to only have one or two purposes. If you've never used one yourself, read up on how they work, what they can do, and also how they absolutely *shouldn't* be used; you're not writing self-help books, but characters engaging in unsafe practices without any kind of acknowledgement or problems can throw your readers out of the scene.

This includes, for example, hot wax play. While readers are generally smart enough to know that throwing a toaster into a bathtub is not a reasonable means of engaging in electrostim, someone who's curious about hot wax but knows very little about it might not think twice about just grabbing some candles out of a drawer and using those. This is dangerous because certain types of wax—often that in household candles—get much, *much* hotter than others, and can result in nasty burns. This is particularly true if the person pouring it on doesn't realize they should hold the candles higher off the skin to give it a chance to cool before it lands.

You don't need to write your scene like a how-to guide by any means. But it is certainly worth keeping in mind that there exist very wrong and very *dangerous* ways to engage in some types of play. If your characters engage in those on page without any kind of issue or concern, then at best, you're going to have readers thrown out of the scene (and likely leaving negative reviews). At worst, someone is going to try it and get hurt.

While authors can't stop readers from trying things they shouldn't, and disclaimers about "y'all, this is fiction" only go so far, we *can* do enough research to at least know whether our characters are engaging in an activity safely and correctly. If they're not, then it should be deliberately and for effect, not because the author couldn't be bothered to read an article or two.

So what if your characters are on a budget? Or they're in a hurry, or they otherwise don't have any toys handy? Fortunately, there are also regular household items that can work for sexy times, such as clothespins and scarves (for blindfolds; generally not recommended for bondage). There are the aforementioned cough drops, peppermints, and ice cubes. Get creative!

In essence, toys are as versatile and have as much story potential as anything, and they're certainly not limited to BDSM.

To recap:

- If one character's limits clash with another's needs, consider toys as a compromise.
- Toys are an amazing way to engage the senses and get those sensory details on the page.
- Toys are not exclusive to BDSM.
- Be safe out there, kids.

CHAPTER 20

WATCH THIS!
VOYEURS & EXHIBITIONISTS

Don't underestimate the heat that voyeurism can bring to your story. After all, sex scenes are, by their very nature, somewhat voyeuristic. While the reader is immersed in the story and the emotions, there is a certain degree of titillation that comes from "watching" the characters in their intimate moment.

In some stories and situations, the writer can capitalize on this—enhancing that voyeurism by turning the characters themselves into voyeurs.

In this scene, Carlene is very new to the idea of her husband, James, being both bisexual and submissive. She's watching while Kent dominates James, and we see the scene through her eyes and feel it through her responses.

Kent cupped James's neck and drew him in. Their lips were nearly touching, but not. Carlene held her breath, waiting for Kent to bridge that last little gap between them.

Holding him still with the hand on his neck,

Kent reached between them and closed his long fingers around James's erection.

James hissed sharply and closed his eyes. "Holy shit."

Carlene's pulse jumped. *Holy shit* was right...

Kent stroked him slowly. "Look right at me. Eyes open. Right on me."

James was struggling to keep his eyes open, but he did as he was told. "Fuck..."

"Not yet." Kent chuckled softly. He leaned in a bit more, their lips just grazing, and added, "I'll fuck you after I'm done fucking *with* you."

James whimpered. His hips started moving in perfect time with Kent's hand.

"You're not going to come until I tell you to." Kent's lips were so, so close to her husband's. "Are you?"

James murmured something Carlene didn't understand.

"Are you?"

"N-no."

"Good." Kent added a subtle twist to his strokes, and grinned at James's frustrated moan. "I don't want you to come yet, because I want you to come while I'm fucking you."

James squeezed his eyes shut. "Jesus..."

"Do you want that, James?" Kent cupped James's cheek with his free hand. "Do you want me to fuck you?"

"Y-yes."

"Wrong answer."

James's eyes flew open. "Huh?"

Kent pulled back, and Carlene lost her breath.

They'd been so close, and she'd been so sure the kiss was inevitable, and now...this?

Kent ran his thumb up and down the side of James's neck. "I'm calling the shots. You do whatever I tell you to. If I want to fuck you, you get on your hands and knees and be fucked. Anything you do, it's because I tell you to."

James swallowed again. His hips were rocking slightly, fucking into Kent's fist, and deep crevices appeared on his forehead as he undoubtedly struggled to comprehend what he was being told. "Anything you want. J-just tell me."

"Good," Kent said softly. "Very good."

James released a ragged breath, and his muscles softened.

"So I'm going to ask again," Kent whispered just loud enough for Carlene to hear, "do you want me to fuck you?"

James slowly ran his tongue across his lips. He studied Kent's eyes, seemed to concentrate hard on them, and finally murmured, "Only if you want to."

Kent smiled, and James shivered. Then Kent shrugged off his jacket, and Carlene's clit tingled. Oh yes, he was wearing his holster. Black. Tight. Emphasizing his chest and his shoulders, plus the butt of the gun sticking out from beneath his arm.

She tried not to fidget, afraid a single creak of the chair would tip them off that she was already more turned on than she should've been.

- Kneel, Mr. President

While the exchange between Kent and James would've been hot from either man's point-of-view, I made a conscious choice to write it this way so that Carlene's arousal could add an extra layer of sexual tension. Ideally, the reader is as on-edge as she is.

Your voyeur need not even be in the same room, or even able to see the act. Sometimes overhearing it is even hotter, because the POV character fills in the visuals in their own mind. In this case, Rhett and Ethan are in the middle of a divorce, but are stuck living together. They've taken in a roommate, Kieran, to keep expenses down, and both are seriously attracted to him.

And tonight, Ethan is taking Kieran to bed.

The house was absolutely silent except for the nearly—but not completely—inaudible sounds they made on their way into Ethan's bedroom.

Ethan's bedroom, which was directly over mine.

I closed my eyes and let out a frustrated breath. One of the selling points of this house was that it was in an exceptionally quiet part of Capitol Hill. Just this once, I wished we'd bought a place right beside the freeway. At least then the roar of traffic would have been enough to drown out the muffled sounds of my ex getting it on with our new roommate.

My eyes tracked across the ceiling, following the sound of their footsteps as if I could see them. Pulling off clothes, stumbling over each other's feet, kissing like only Ethan knew how to kiss.

I shivered. It didn't matter how or why we'd split or how we felt about each other, the fact remained that no one kissed like Ethan Mallory. *Oh, Kieran, you lucky son of a bitch.*

The lips were only the beginning. Right about now, Kieran was probably discovering just how many erogenous zones Ethan could find on someone's neck, or what his perpetually stubbled jaw felt like when skin brushed skin, or what Ethan's voice felt like when he moaned into a deep kiss. I ran my tongue stud along my teeth, remembering the way Ethan would tease it with the tip of his tongue.

Just wait until you find out what else his mouth can do, lad.

They stopped moving. I could hear nothing except for the beating of my own heart, but my mind's eye filled in everything that was probably going on. If I knew Ethan, he was anything but silent right then, kissing his way up and down Kieran's neck while whispering in great detail all the ways he'd make him beg for more.

And if I knew Ethan, he wasn't exaggerating. Whatever he said he would do, he did. Promises of a rough, hard fuck or a long, spine-melting blowjob, even a gentle, oiled massage that would no doubt lead to much more. I could almost feel Ethan's lips and voice against my neck as he breathed all his promises.

The distant, muffled sound of a belt buckle made me shiver. Clothes hit the floor; jeans, I guessed, if I could hear it that clearly. Footsteps moved above me, then bedsprings creaked softly.

I closed my eyes again. I wanted to be angry, I wanted to be jealous, but just the thought of either of those men, naked and horny, made me want to be *there*. And whether I liked it or not, my body wanted to be there too.

Reaching under the covers, I closed my hand around my cock and stroked slowly, barely even breathing so as not to drown out the faint sounds from upstairs.

- The Distance Between Us

We don't see what's going on between Ethan and Kieran, but we feel it through Rhett's voyeuristic experience. Via Rhett, we can imagine everything they're doing, and we also feel Rhett's arousal and frustration. Showing the sex scene between Ethan and Kieran would've been hot, yes, but Rhett's POV adds another layer of tension and heat. The book is also exclusively in his POV, so this is a solution for showing the reader Ethan and Kieran together while still staying in Rhett's head.

As another example of voyeurism and exhibitionism, Ryan's biggest fantasy is a gangbang with some strangers. His Dom, Misha, makes it happen, and the scene is split between their POVs, so we get Ryan's POV as the exhibitionist at the center of the gangbang as well as Misha's as the voyeur.

From Ryan's POV...

The two heading toward my groin got there, and... Whoa. One of them teased my balls with the tip of his tongue, and the other took my dick between his lips, easing down a little at a time.

"Oh my... Holy fuck..." I heard myself moan. Was that the first time I'd made a sound since we'd started? Did they think I wasn't enjoying myself? "Fucking—"

Lips claimed mine, and to hell with talking. Or trying to keep tabs on hands and dicks and mouths. I lost track of who was who. I didn't know their names anyway, but it wouldn't have mattered if I did. A hand caressed my abs. Another closed my fingers around his—or another guy's?—thick erection.

I didn't even know where my own hands were. When I wasn't stroking a dick, I felt around and rubbed, massaged, caressed skin when I found it. Whose? Who cared? No matter which way I reached, I was touching beautiful naked men. And had Misha hand-picked these guys for their ability to kiss? Not one of them was a bad kisser. Or even a mediocre one. The mental image of him making out with them in his office to make sure they knew what they were doing... Oh God. *Yeah.*

Every once in a while, I'd open my eyes and shift them toward the side of the room, and as soon as my gaze would lock with Misha's, all the crazy sensations intensified. Being in bed with a bunch of men I didn't know was hot. But being watched intently by Misha? Holy fuck. I'd never thought of myself as an exhibitionist. Maybe when he was involved, I was. Especially when he had that obvious hard-on tenting his tailored slacks.

- The Master Will Appear

And from Misha's...

Ryan was utterly gorgeous like that. Sweating, panting, surrounded by naked men. And when things had been at their most frantic, when he'd been taking cocks every place he could... This was Ryan's fantasy, but it was amazingly hot for me to watch.

Even better, I knew exactly what each man had been feeling. Taking Ryan's cock when he came. Sliding in and out of Ryan's mouth. Holding onto his hips and thrusting into him until he nearly sobbed with pleasure.

The hottest thing of all was watching Ryan melt in their hands. His pupils were blown and his body was boneless, and his face and throat were flushed with arousal. Every time a cock moved in his mouth or in his ass, he squirmed with palpable ecstasy.

And though I knew what every one of *them* felt, and not one of them knew what I felt when I was with Ryan. What it was like to have him kneeling at my feet, eyes wide with total surrender, his back marked from my strokes and his chest wet with my semen. None of them knew the strain in his expression when I kept his climax out of his reach or the pure relief when I let him come.

I shivered in my seat, thrilling at watching him take more pleasure than he could bear from these five men and yet still keeping some of it for myself. Knowing there were things we would do when we were alone that were ours and only ours. Things that were *mine.*

- *The Master Will Appear*

These snippets will be revisited in the chapter on group sex, so I'm just going to focus on the exhibitionist/voyeur aspect. Much like the scenes above from *The Distance Between Us* and *Kneel, Mr. President*, the voyeurism adds another layer of experience and arousal. Both POV characters are getting off on watching each other—in Ryan's case, watching Misha watch him. Even when Misha isn't being physically stimulated, he's intensely turned on from watching his partner and remembering how it feels to be the one doing those things to Ryan. The scene is whetting his appetite for sex with Ryan, and is also deeply fulfilling because he's successfully helping Ryan live out a fantasy. Throughout the scene, Misha simply sits there and watches, but we can feel all the physical and emotional responses he has to what's playing out in front of him.

Finally, voyeurism does not need to include more than just your main characters. If they trust each other enough, they can video or film themselves together. Or they can have sex in front of a mirror or under a mirrored ceiling so they can watch.

Do keep in mind that not every story will lend itself to voyeurism. Some people don't enjoy watching themselves. For others, having someone else watch would be deeply violating. There is the issue of consent. In this day and age, particularly with cameras everywhere and privacy becoming a thing of the past, many people fiercely guard what privacy they still possess. This can make it challenging for a reader to fully engage and enjoy a story of voyeurism if it's not explicitly consensual.

And even without privacy or consent issues, sometimes it's just not the right vibe for the story. Keep these things in mind when you're setting up a voyeur or exhibitionist element.

To recap:

- Voyeurism can add tension and arousal to an already hot scene.
- It can be a solution when you want to show two characters besides your POV character having sex.
- It can be as simple as the characters watching themselves in front of a mirror.
- Be mindful of consent and privacy.

CHAPTER 21

MÉNAGE A HOW MANY?
GROUP SEX

Sex with one person is fun, so it only gets exponentially more fun with every person you add, right?

Well... kind of.

Threesomes, foursomes, fiveways, orgies, gangbangs—they're complicated. Complicated enough that this chapter is broken up into two sections—emotions and the physical. Well, technically two and a half sections, since I gave double penetration its own header.

Let's start with emotions.

Part I
Emotions

Before we get into the logistics, let's talk about *why* you're writing a group scene. As we discussed in the beginning of the book, sex scenes can (and should, in romantic fiction) have an emotional component as well as being hot and sexy.

Are your characters involved in a polyamorous relationship? Do you have two couples hooking up for a night of fun? Is this a one-time thing where a couple brings in a third? There are endless scenarios that can lead to more than two people getting naked together.

Maybe your couple is adding a third for a night or for the long term. Or two couples are playing together. Or a few people decide to jump into bed and have a hot night together.

Maybe you have a male/female couple, and one partner has an unexplored bisexual side. This can actually be a bit of a minefield, too. There are people out there who've been burned—sometimes more than once—by couples who brought them in as a third so one or both could experiment with bisexuality. Afterward, with the bi-curiosity was sated, the third was unceremoniously dismissed.

If your characters are bringing in a third person to explore some bisexuality, be mindful of the possibilities for rejection, hurt, and feeling used. Similarly, the existing partner might feel threatened—will my partner leave me for this shiny, new person? Or maybe they'll decide they're gay instead of bi? What if the new person falls in love with my partner?

Regardless of the sexualities of everyone involved, a threesome, foursome, or whateversome can potentially be a catalyst for some serious jealousy and insecurity. Maybe your character thought it would be hot to see their partner with someone else, but when it actually happens, they're jealous and territorial instead of aroused. Or maybe the new partner has a bigger cock. Or can give their partner bigger orgasms with less effort. Or has a hotter body or more stamina. In my book *Kneel, Mr. President*, Carlene Broderick is considering sharing her husband with his best friend and former lover, but she's got some reservations:

Her thoughts drifted to Kent. The man wasn't the ripped, tanned SEAL he used to be. Some of his old injuries had slowed him down, and he wasn't quite as religious about working out as he had been during their military years. Neither was James. Instead of six-packs, they each had smooth, flat abs these days. James had lost some muscle tone, so she imagined Kent had too, but they were hardly flabby. They were battle-scarred, graying, and both bastards could grace the cover of a men's fitness magazine if they wanted to.

Especially since neither had carried and given birth to three kids. Two at the same time.

As she stripped down to a T-shirt and panties, Carlene didn't dare look at herself in the mirror. No sense comparing herself to the guys. Specifically, the guy whose body *hadn't* been ravaged by time and pregnancy *and* whose name her husband kept saying in his sleep.

- Kneel, Mr. President

Now imagine actually putting her in the bedroom with those two men, and you can see how some serious insecurity can develop as she compares herself to Kent, and on top of that, she worries she's fighting him for her husband's affection.

Remember, emotions don't have to be entirely rational to be real. Sex makes people vulnerable, which can make those not-completely-rational emotions run wild. Dig into those emotions!

A ménage situation—whether it's just sexual or it's polyamorous—is also a place where positive emotions can happen. Maybe your character realizes they don't want anyone else except their partner, for example.

Or, if your characters are involved in a poly relationship, a group scene can have the same effect a one-on-one scene does with a couple—bonding them and deepening their intimacy. For example, in *The Best Laid Plans*, my three characters—Gabe, Shahid, and Kendra—experience a few bumps before they realize their three-way arrangement works. Shahid is gay, and has always had some uneasiness about being married to a bisexual man, but he's quickly warming up to the idea of Kendra being a regular fixture in their bed:

Gabe rolled Kendra onto her back, and she wrapped her legs around him. For a long moment, all I did was stare, watching them, drinking in the sight of those two beautiful people kissing on top of the sheets. He still took my breath away after all these years, but seeing him tangled up with her, with soft feminine curves emphasizing his harder angles, was erotic in a way I'd never imagined. His hands traced the swell of her hips, and my mouth watered.

Then she spread her legs a little farther apart, and as his hips made a slow, curving forward motion, she gasped. He moaned. I shivered. As if watching them kiss hadn't been hot enough, watching him ride her slowly was unbelievable. The absence of jealousy tightening my chest or coiling in the pit of my stomach was conspicuous—I really had gotten used to this, hadn't I?

Gotten used to it? Hardly. I *loved* it. Everything about it. The sounds Kendra made, the way Gabe's brow furrowed and his muscles quivered from the exertion of moving so slowly, the way their bodies seemed to just fit together. Jealousy had long since left the building because I knew Gabe would be all mine later—and he'd be *insatiable*—and these two would hardly leave me feeling neglected.

- The Best Laid Plans

So, when you're writing a ménage scene, keep in mind that emotions can run seriously hot as the population in the bedroom increases. Know your characters, their reasons for (and possibly reservations against) additional people, and how it will affect everyone in the moment and after.

Part II
Physical

The thing is, sex is a lot of physical work. And when there's more people involved, it's a lot more work. If your characters are all into each other, it's one thing. But if, for example, your female character is having a threesome with two straight dudes, she's going to be *busy*. Once Dude 1 has gotten off, he might bow out for a breather, leaving her to do her thing with Dude 2. But then once Dude 2 has gotten off, it's entirely possible Dude 1 is ready to get back in the game. When does *she* get to take a breather?

The body has its limits.

And speaking of bodies, it can be very easy to lose track of body parts while writing a ménage scene. See the chapter on choreography for additional tips for this.

Writing in a close POV (typically first person or third limited) can work to your advantage. Your POV character won't know precisely what everyone is doing or thinking at a given moment. The author should know, but the character —and the reader—doesn't necessarily need to.

Incidentally, this can make it fun because a person might be (for example) going down on one character, and then realize another character is starting to penetrate them, and they might not be completely certain who that is. Assuming everyone is on the same page about consent—i.e., it's understood that this character is game for being penetrated by anyone involved—it can make the scene quite hot.

For example, in the voyeurism chapter, I mentioned and quoted a scene from *The Master Will Appear* where Misha has arranged to fulfill Ryan's fantasy of a gangbang. Ryan, the POV character in the first half of the scene, is in bed with five men he doesn't know:

Lips claimed mine, and to hell with talking. Or trying to keep tabs on hands and dicks and mouths. I lost track of who was who. I didn't know their names anyway, but it wouldn't have mattered if I did. A hand caressed my abs. Another closed my fingers around his—or another guy's?—thick erection.

I didn't even know where my own hands were. When I wasn't stroking a dick, I felt around and rubbed, massaged, caressed skin when I found it.

Whose? Who cared? No matter which way I reached, I was touching beautiful naked men.

- The Master Will Appear

This alleviates the issue of trying to keep the reader abreast of every single body part, and also gives the scene a somewhat delirious feeling.

This can still work from the perspective of an observer, too. From the second half of the same scene, this time in Misha's point of view:

The men who hadn't come yet were still rock-hard, and hands and mouths lazily paid attention to their cocks, but no one seemed to be in any hurry for the moment.

Ryan was utterly gorgeous like that. Sweating, panting, surrounded by naked men. And when things had been at their most frantic, when he'd been taking cocks every place he could... This was Ryan's fantasy, but it was amazingly hot for me to watch.

Even better, I knew exactly what each man had been feeling. Taking Ryan's cock when he came. Sliding in and out of Ryan's mouth. Holding onto his hips and thrusting into him until he nearly sobbed with pleasure.

The hottest thing of all was watching Ryan melt in their hands. His pupils were blown and his body was boneless, and his face and throat were flushed with arousal. Every time a cock moved in his mouth or in his ass, he squirmed with palpable ecstasy.

And though I knew what every one of them felt, and not one of them knew what I felt when I was with Ryan. What it was like to have him kneeling at my feet, eyes wide with total surrender, his back marked from my strokes and his chest wet with my semen. None of them knew the strain in his expression when I kept his climax out of his reach or the pure relief when I let him come.

I shivered in my seat, thrilling at watching him take more pleasure than he could bear from these five men and yet still keeping some of it for myself. Knowing there were things we would do when we were alone that were ours and only ours. Things that were mine.

- The Master Will Appear

Notice there isn't a ton of focus on which body parts are where, who's doing what, etc. The focus is on responses and feelings, so your reader doesn't need a diagram to keep track of parts. But it still doesn't hurt for *you* to have that diagram while you're writing so you know what's going on.

And as long as we're trying not to lose track of anything...

Pronouns can also be tricky in group sex scenes, and this goes hand in hand with name repetition. I once wrote an all-male foursome in third person, and I pretty much wanted to throw the book out the window by the third paragraph just because the names and pronouns were making my eyes cross. If you're struggling with this aspect, it doesn't mean you're doing it wrong—just having that many bodies tangled up is going to make things challenging.

To lessen the name repetition and pronoun confusion:

- If you haven't already begun writing, consider your POV. I personally prefer first person anyway, but I find it is especially useful when this particular issue comes up.
- Resist the urge to do a body part play-by-play. Often, when a writer is struggling with pronouns/name repetition in a sex scene, this is the core of the issue—focusing too much on what each body part is doing to another body part. Concentrate on what your POV character is feeling as much as what they're doing.
- Keep a tight focus.

It'll still feel a lot like you're spinning plates, but you'll keep better track of the plates. Keep in mind that writing a group sex scene is a lot like writing a car chase scene. In your head, it probably plays out like a movie, but *on the page*, your focus will be much tighter. While you can see the entire scene, your character can only see from where they are sitting. Or, well, lying. In a way, this makes things easier because you can just concentrate on what your character is aware of.

It can also make things much more complicated because you're trying to portray a big theatrical scene with only one camera. Imagine one of those huge, chaotic car chases in a movie, entirely shot from *one* camera in *one* car, and you can see how difficult that would be. Incidentally, this is why I hate writing car chase scenes, but with sex scenes, it actually simplifies things a bit.

Yeah, you'd still be wise to plot out the logistics.

But at least you don't have to worry about that jersey barrier coming up on the left.

Part II.V
Double Penetration

I know, that's not really how Roman numerals work, but here we are.

As long as we're talking about the physical logistics of group sex, I think we'd be remiss if we didn't talk about double penetration. In the erotica I've read, it's not uncommon for group sex to include double penetration, and it's something that I decided needed its own section.

So. Double penetration. This can mean vaginal/anal, double anal, or double vaginal. And we know it's possible— we've seen it in pornos!

Except... here's the thing with porn: just because it can be done, and just because it looks hot for the camera, doesn't mean it's particularly *comfortable*. See the chapter on porn.

It can certainly be done. It can be fun, too. But you might be hard-pressed to hold onto your reader's suspension of disbelief if your new-to-bottoming character is happily getting anally double-stuffed but two exceptionally huge cocks and/or toys.

The thing is, even single penetration is a snug fit. Pushing twice as much into the same orifice is going to take some work, especially if it's going to be enjoyable for the owner of said orifice. Think about how much someone has to relax in order to comfortably bottom. Now add a second penis to the mix. If anyone tries to rush, someone's going to be in pain.

Similarly, if a character is being penetrated both anally and vaginally, there is some serious potential for pain. When they're taking two penises (or toys, or whatever), there's a relatively thin—and quite sensitive—piece of tissue separating those two orifices and, by extension, the two penises. If they're both jackhammering away, there's a good chance that piece of tissue is getting pinched.

Did that make your nether regions clench? Mine too.

But... in all the pornos, double penetration is done hard and fast! Yep, and this is one of those rare (LOL) places where porn and real life diverge. In porn, double penetration is usually performed as vigorously as single penetration. In reality—at least according to the dozens of articles and blogs I've read on the subject—the name of the game is *go slow, at least at first.*

It's entirely possible they go slow at first in a porno too, but it's very easy to edit a scene and make it look like they've gone from zero to sixty in a couple of seconds.

So is this all a long-winded way of saying that double penetration has no place in erotic fiction? Absolutely not. In fact, a double penetration scene can be hot, not to mention rich in those emotional components I've been talking about throughout this book. Particularly if this is a romance story, and even in erotica, one would generally assume the characters have a certain amount of affection for each other. And trust, for that matter. If they're all willing to indulge in a scene like this, you have a *golden opportunity* as the author to demonstrate that trust and affection.

You can show...

- ...the bottom being nervous, but trusting that their partners won't hurt them.
- ...the tops being laser-focused on the bottom,

watching for signs of discomfort and doing everything they can—from speaking in soothing voices to using generous amounts of lube—to keep the bottom comfortable.
- …the tops communicating (verbally or otherwise) with each other.
- …the tops taking their time, and eventually picking up speed as the bottom telegraphs (or outright says) they're ready.
- …the bottom deciding it's too much and safewording out. (Which then provides loads of opportunity for the tops to show if they're truly committed to keeping the bottom happy)
- …the bottom continuing despite the discomfort, and one or both tops deciding to stop.

As you can see, a double penetration scene can be so much more than just something hot and unusual. Bring in an emotional component, and mind the logistics so your characters aren't getting hurt and your readers aren't cringing, and you have the makings of a sexy, memorable, and possibly even poignant scene.

Or it can just be a ridiculously hot scene between three people. It doesn't have to be anything more than that. It just goes back to what we talked about in the sex on the beach chapter—your reader might not give it much thought, and might take the fantasy at face value without worrying about the logistics, but there's a good chance at least *some* will think "wait, that sounds kind of painful…"

Double penetration is certainly possible. For some, it can be a lot of fun. Just be mindful of how experienced and comfortable your character is, and how much stretching and contorting is involved. There are actual tutorials online for how to engage in double penetration, and I'd recommend reading several of those to get a feel for what's truly involved.

To recap...

- Group sex has more complex logistics.
- It can also cause a lot of complex emotions that might not crop up in monogamous situations.
- Planning, tracking, and diagramming a scene isn't sexy... but the resulting scene will be!
- When you're playing with things like double penetration, get creative and have fun... but carefully consider what might pull your readers out of the scene.

RESEARCH

Let me preface this by saying that if you've never published anything spicy before, you may be wholly unprepared for the sheer number of people who will, upon learning you write such material, volunteer to help you with research. Usually with a suggestive leer and a waggled eyebrow. Responding with an earnest request to assist you in learning the finer points of sounding—especially accompanied by a graphic explanation of exactly what sounding entails—is extraordinarily effective at dissuading many of these generous individuals. Your mileage may vary, but there it is.

To be serious, writing sex does require some intimate knowledge of sexuality, the human body, sexual practices, etc. This book is certainly not going to teach you all the finer points of every specific fetish, practice, position, sensation, toy, etc., and most of us will end up writing at least a few scenes that are out of our own wheelhouses.

Thus... research.

The obvious answer is to try it. If you've got a partner who's game, or it's something you can do solo... Well, you know what to do. If you don't have a partner, or you're not comfortable broaching the subject of such a thing, there are also toys.

But you may not be comfortable trying or able to try everything, and that's perfectly fine. It is 100% acceptable to write sex scenes involving things you have no desire to do yourself or that you are unable to do for any reason. (And as an aside, you should never have to explain or justify why you can't or won't try something you write about. Ever.)

So beyond trying it yourself, the next option is asking people. If you're shy or don't know someone you're comfortable asking, there are internet forums out there where people discuss sex and fetishes, and they need not know your name or any details beyond "I'm curious about X." Of course the internet is a bit of a free for all, and as with anything, there is plenty of misinformation on this subject out there, so you'll need to engage in a lot of critical thinking to separate the wheat from the chaff. When in doubt... ask questions.

The internet is also teeming with blogs and articles that address these things. Since not everything on the internet is accurate, I recommend reading multiple sources to find a consensus. That's what I did when I wanted to write a scene involving a single tail (basically a whip). I searched for articles and blog posts written by people who had actually experienced the single tail (either giving or receiving), and read as much as I could get my hands on.

And that brings up another point: I highly recommend researching from the perspective of someone who wants to engage in a particular practice, not write about it.

If you want to write about flying a plane, you research how to fly a plane, pilot experiences, etc., not how to *write* about it. Approach sex scenes the same way. Do you want to write about bondage? Read books, blogs, etc., intended for people who are into bondage.

That doesn't mean you should avoid information on writing such scenes. I firmly believe things like that are helpful, especially for people who are just starting out—that's why I wrote this book! But you'll gain a much richer and more nuanced understanding of a subject if you *also* learn about a subject from the perspective of people who do it in the real-world.

For that matter, you might also glean things you never would have considered before, which can make your book even better. As an example, while doing some research about Dom/sub dynamics, I stumbled across an article on Emma Austin's blog about a Dom with ADHD. It went into some detail about how domination focuses her Dom, which got me thinking about what it would be like to write such a character. This led to the Dom in *Extra Whip* having ADHD, which led to some interesting dynamics between him, his husband, and their third. (This article is linked in the bibliography at the end of this book.)

It was admittedly disappointing to take kink off the table after I'd been looking forward to it all day, but I would never complain. As much as I wanted, another night of pain and submission, no way in hell would I ask for it when Will was in this state of mind. He'd be able to focus, and he'd be able to give me what I needed, but it would be extra taxing on him when he was already having a day like this.

So tonight, Kelly and I would take care of him. I

didn't mind at all. Maybe it wasn't pain, sex, or bondage, but I liked this kind of submission too. The quieter, gentler version where I was at my Dom's beck and call for anything he needed or wanted.

When Kelly arrived, he went in to say hello to Will, then joined me again in the kitchen. Glancing over his shoulder, he said, "So, he's okay, right?"

"Oh yeah. He's fine. But when his ADHD gets going, he can just get really scattered, which makes it hard as hell to get anything done. Then he gets frustrated, and—I mean, he says it's like analysis paralysis. Where he's hyper-focusing and overthinking, but he can't actually *do* anything, and then everything kills his concentration. He gets overstimulated, and..." I shook my head. "It's just not a good time to ask him to be a Dom because his brain is already overtaxed, he's already overstimulated, and he won't enjoy it at all."

- Extra Whip

Had I just been researching how to write Dom/sub dynamics, I likely would have missed this unique take from someone writing about her own lived experience, and my character would have been less interesting.

To recap:

- Try what you're comfortable and able to try.
- If you're comfortable, ask people who have experience.

- Use websites, message boards, and the like to connect with experienced people.
- Read, read, read.
- Focus more on researching how to *do* something than how to *write* it.

To get you started, there is a selection of recommended books in the bibliography.

A FEW FINAL WORDS

As I bring this book to a close, I hope I've made the process of writing sex scenes a little clearer and maybe even a little easier for you. Much of what I included here boils down to just being mindful and conscious of the choices you make. Your sex scene and its components can have any effect you want, but I strongly believe those effects should be—yep, let's say it together—deliberate and for effect. By doing this, you'll avoid scenes that are dull, repetitive, unintentionally hilarious, or wince-inducing.

If nothing else, I hope I've conveyed that the vast majority of sex scenes have far more potential than many people realize. I found this to be incredibly freeing, and it made writing sex scenes into less of a chore and more of what every scene should be—an opportunity to show far, far more than just squishy bits and O-faces.

Go forth, and may your sex scenes be hot, memorable, and free of sand.

L.A. Witt

RECOMMENDED READING & BIBLIOGRAPHY

Websites

- The Submissive Guide - https://submissiveguide.com/

- Love Emma Austin – BDSM Blog: https://www.loveemmaaustin.com/latest-1/what-its-like-to-have-sex-with-someone-who-has-adhd

Books

- The Anal Sex Position Guide (Tristan Taormino)
- The Whole Lesbian Sex Book: A Passionate Guide for All of Us (Felicia Newman & Kaylee West)
- Screw the Roses, Send Me the Thorns: The Romance and Sexual Sorcery of Sadomasochism (Molly Devon & Philip Miller)

- Gay New York: Gender, Urban Culture, and
  the Making of the Gay Male World, 1890-1940
  (George Chauncey)

LIST OF REFERENCED WORKS & AUTHORS

Price, Jordan Castillo

- https://jordancastilloprice.com/
- Spook Squad (PsyCop, book 5)
- Criss Cross (PsyCop, book 2)

Zabo, Anna

- https://annazabo.com/
- Cinnamon Roll

Hayward, L.J.

- http://www.ljhayward.com/
- Death and the Devil series

Referenced books written by the author
(written as L.A. Witt unless otherwise noted)
http://www.gallagherwitt.com/

- A Chip In His Shoulder
- BCC (written as Lauren Gallagher)
- Bouncing Back
- Conduct Unbecoming
- Extra Whip
- Hitman vs. Hitman (co-written with Cari Z)
- I'll Show You Mine (written as Lauren Gallagher)
- Just Hear Me
- Kneel, Mr. President (written as Lauren Gallagher)
- Luca, Cole, Bryce, & Hunter (Gentlemen of the Emerald City 1, 2, 3, & 6, respectively)
- Risky Behavior (co-written with Cari Z)
- Rookie Mistake (co-written with Anna Zabo)
- Stuck Landing (written as Lauren Gallagher)
- The Best Laid Plans (written as Lauren Gallagher)
- The Master Will Appear
- The Right to Remain
- The Venetian and the Rum Runner
- The Walls Between Hearts
- When Yvette Moved In (written as Lauren Gallagher)
- Who's Your Daddy? (written as Lauren Gallagher)
- You Had One Job (co-written with Cari Z)

For more books by L.A. Witt, please visit

http://www.gallagherwitt.com

Romance * Suspense

Contemporary * Historical * Sports * Military

Titles Include

Rookie Mistake (written with Anna Zabo)

Scoreless Game (written with Anna Zabo)

The Hitman vs. Hitman Series (written with Cari Z)

The Bad Behavior Series (written with Cari Z)

The Gentlemen of the Emerald City Series

The Anchor Point Series

The Husband Gambit

Name From a Hat Trick

After December

Brick Walls

The Venetian and the Rum Runner

If The Seas Catch Fire

...and many, many more!

ABOUT THE AUTHOR

L.A. Witt is a romance and suspense author who has at last given up the exciting nomadic lifestyle of the military spouse (read: her husband finally retired). She now resides in Pittsburgh, where the potholes are determined to eat her car and her cats are endlessly taunted by a disrespectful squirrel named Moose. In her spare time, she can be found painting in her art room or destroying her voice at a Pittsburgh Penguins game.

Website: www.gallagherwitt.com
    Email: gallagherwitt@gmail.com
    Twitter: @GallagherWitt

NOTES

5. MOVIES ARE YOUR FRIEND

1. In the US, an NC-17 rating means no one under the age of 17 is permitted. This is often seen as a kiss of death for movies.
2. I wouldn't consider professional porn to be all that helpful because the facial expressions, vocalizations, etc., tend to be heavily scripted, exaggerated, and more for the benefit of the camera and viewer than the partner.

6. BOW-CHICKA-THAT DOESN'T LOOK FUN

1. Pretty sure that doesn't exist, but if it does, I could totally see them mandating bastardized reverse cowgirl.

6. DON'T EXAGGERATE THE SIZE OF YOUR FISH

1. King BM. Average-Size Erect Penis: Fiction, Fact, and the Need for Counseling. J Sex Marital Ther. 2021;47(1):80-89. doi: 10.1080/0092623X.2020.1787279. Epub 2020 Jul 15. PMID: 32666897.
2. How deep is a vagina? What to know. Medically reviewed by Cynthia Cobb, DNP, APRN, WHNP-BC, FAANP — By Rachel Nall, MSN, CRNA on January 12, 2020 https://www.medicalnewstoday.com/articles/321220

8. YES OR NO?

1. No disrespect toward readers/writers of Regency. Simply expressing just how much of an impact that book had on me.

14. TAKE A DEEP BREATH AND RELAX

1. If you *want* to make them cringe or wince, fine. Do it deliberately. I'm talking about doing it unintentionally.

17. THERE IS SEX AFTER 25...

1. Hat tip to Leta Blake for this term instead of May-December, which always makes it sound like the older character is on Death's door.